# Into Your Hands

## Planning a Catholic funeral, readings and prayers

*taken from the Order of Christian Funerals*

Decani Books

## Acknowledgements

Published by Decani, Oak House, 70 High Street, Brandon, Suffolk IP27 0AU
First published in 1999
Second printing, incorporating additions, 2006
Third printing 2011

ISBN 10:  1 900 31404 5
ISBN 13:  978-1-900314-04-6

Printed by AbbeyHine Limited, Lamdin Road, Bury St Edmunds, Suffolk, IP32 6NU.
www.abbeyhine.co.uk

# Into Your Hands

## planning a Catholic funeral, readings and prayers

*taken from the Order of Christian Funerals*

*In sure and certain hope of the resurrection*

# Contents

# Planning the Funeral

This book has two purposes: to help people plan a funeral, and to assist a lay person who may be asked to lead prayers or a service in a home or hospital.

## Why Funeral Rites?

Christians celebrate funeral rites to offer worship and thanksgiving to God, the author of all life. We pray for the deceased, and support the bereaved. A funeral should not be an isolated moment, but part of the life of a community in which people care for each other.

Being involved in preparing and planning someone's funeral – even our own – can be part of coming to terms with death. It also enables people to become engaged in the funeral liturgy itself and allows them to be touched by the occasion. The planning can take place in conjunction with prayers or a service in the family home.

The notes which follow presume that the reader is preparing someone else's funeral. If you are planning your own funeral, however, you will also need to ask yourself the questions posed here. You may be considering whether to purchase a pre-paid funeral package. If so, ensure that your preferred options are accommodated in it. Some plans, for instance, do not include a service in church as well as burial or cremation.

Actual funeral practice varies considerably, and the Church provides several options from which we can choose freely. There is greater flexibility and involvement possible than we sometimes imagine.

# What are the options?

Formal reception of the body into church the night before the funeral is still a common Catholic practice, though less so than previously. Recent years have also seen a drift towards the single service held in the cemetery chapel or at the crematorium.

In the face of this trend the Church is drawing our attention to the human reality of the funeral as a journey: for the one who has died, the mourners, and for the parish community. The model for this is the Easter journey of Jesus Christ from death to resurrection. This is why we are encouraged to celebrate the funeral in three stages or movements: vigil, funeral liturgy, and committal.

### 1. Vigil

For many people, the idea of a vigil is something new. Yet this helpful service is to be encouraged. It is the principal rite celebrated between the death and the funeral itself. As the first stage of the farewell journey, its mood is one of quiet support which helps to prepare the bereaved for the final leave-taking.

The Vigil may be held in the home of the deceased, the funeral home, or in another suitable place, for instance a hospital chapel. However, it may also be celebrated in church, possibly in conjunction with the reception of the body (though this may take place at the start of the funeral liturgy itself). Even in church, this vigil takes the form of a liturgy of the word of God, or Evening Prayer. Where there is a delay between the death and the funeral, the vigil may be repeated as necessary and adapted according to the circumstances.

### 2. Funeral Liturgy

This is the main liturgical celebration of the Christian community for the deceased person and is usually held in church. Two forms are possible: a funeral Mass, or a funeral liturgy outside Mass. Whether to celebrate Mass or not is discussed below.

### 3. Committal

The rite of committal usually follows on immediately from the funeral liturgy. This final act of leave-taking is celebrated at the graveside or at the crematorium. Whether to have a burial or a cremation is discussed below.

## Making the Best Choice

While we are encouraged to celebrate a funeral over these three stages (vigil, funeral liturgy, and committal), for a variety of good reasons this model is not always possible or appropriate to the circumstances.

The family may not wish to have a vigil either in the home or in church. In this case, the body will be received into church at the start of the funeral liturgy itself and the service will lead directly to the committal. The funeral may even comprise a single act of worship either in the cemetery chapel or at the crematorium.

Many combinations of funeral rite are possible.

# Reception of the body

The first point to note is that the vigil is not tied to church, and the reception of the body into church is not a necessary part of it. Reception can take place as part of the funeral liturgy itself, or the body may be brought to church in advance of the vigil or funeral liturgy. This allows three possible formats. These are shown on the diagram opposite.

In the diagram, a horizontal line indicates the following (or a different) day:

| 1 | 2 | 3 |
|---|---|---|
| | | Reception |
| Vigil | Vigil with reception | Vigil |
| | | |
| Funeral with reception | Funeral | Funeral |
| Committal | Committal | Committal |

# Time of day

A second point is that the funeral liturgy itself is not tied to any particular hour of the day. It may be that most of the mourners are better able to attend an evening service, or that a priest is able to celebrate Mass only in the evening. In such cases, you might hold a liturgy of the word of God, or Morning Prayer, on the following day, and this will lead directly to the committal. This format can still include a vigil:

| |
|---|
| Vigil |
| |
| Funeral with reception |
| |
| Liturgy of the Word |
| Committal |

# Mass

The third and perhaps the most important question is whether to have Mass or not. The Church encourages a Mass since the eucharist is the memorial celebration of Christ's own death and resurrection. However, while the eucharist is our central liturgy, it is not always the best option for a funeral. Moreover a funeral outside Mass, like a wedding outside Mass, is a full Catholic liturgy, not something second rate.

Factors to consider include the following:

- Was the deceased person a Mass-goer? Are the bereaved?
- Has the deceased person expressed a preference or left instructions?
- Will there be a large proportion of non-Catholics present?
- Can the funeral take place at the hour of the regular weekday Mass?

All these point to the following question: What percentage of the congregation will be able to take an active part in the eucharistic liturgy?

Where the circumstances suggest a funeral service, the family could be invited to the parish Mass on the day of the funeral, or a special Mass may be arranged sometime afterwards.

Note that on certain key feast days of the Church a funeral Mass is not permitted, for instance Ascension Day and Maundy Thursday. Also, if your priest is not available, a funeral service conducted by your parish deacon may be preferable to a Mass celebrated by a priest you do not know, brought in for the occasion.

Thus, a further two options suggest themselves. As before, the reception of the body may take place as part of the funeral liturgy itself, or the body may be brought to church in advance of the vigil or funeral liturgy:

| Vigil | Vigil |
|---|---|
| Parish Mass Funeral Committal | Funeral Committal |
| | Memorial Mass |

## Burial or cremation

The fourth area to consider is the choice between burial and cremation. Here are some thoughts to help reach a decision.

Burial has always been part of the Christian funeral. Tradition has given us a rich ceremony, using prayers and symbols drawn from Scripture, focusing on the burial of Jesus.

Burial allows people to face the reality of death. The coffin is lowered into the ground. You can express your farewell by sprinkling earth or holy water on to the coffin. You leave, having 'settled' the dead person in a special place.

Cremation is relatively new for Catholics, and there has not been time to develop traditions like those connected with burial. However, in the crematorium it is still possible to bid farewell in a dignified way.

You may lay a hand on the coffin or sprinkle it with holy water. This can be done during the service or on leaving the chapel. The withdrawal of the coffin from sight in the cremation service is an echo of the lowering of the coffin into the ground at burial.

Cremation should not be the end of the farewell process. It may indeed leave you with a sense of incompleteness. Interring the ashes sometime after the cremation can help bring the natural cycle to completion: earth to earth, ashes to ashes, dust to dust.

Because ashes should be treated with the same reverence shown to the body of the dead person, it is important to give them a resting place. Your parish (or the cemetery) may have a garden of remembrance where ashes can be reverently returned to the earth. This provides a focus for the parish's sense of communion with the departed, who are still members of the family of faith. The community will pray there and you have a place of memory.

The choice between burial and cremation may involve more practical considerations. The dead person may have expressed a preference or left written instructions as to the committal. Local and family customs will be a factor also. Depending on the type of grave chosen, you will need to consider the question of its upkeep in addition to the initial expenditure on purchase.

While the requirements for burial at sea are not covered in this book, it is a legitimate option which some people may wish to consider.

Increasing concern for the care of the environment is leading people to consider newer options. These include woodland graves, which some cemeteries now provide as a natural setting for burial. A fully biodegradable coffin or a woollen shroud may be used in place of the chipboard and plastics used in most modern coffins. In making a choice of container and wrapping for the dead body, you should bear in mind the likely time between death and the funeral.

In all this, the key issue is how best to make the farewell for the dead, how best to honour the dead person, and how best to hold them in memory.

## After the Funeral

A funeral is often followed by a reception. This may be the first opportunity for some of the mourners to meet and console one another. So apart from its practical function, the reception can itself be part of the leave-taking. It can set the seal on the liturgy and allow emotional release, since people may be both tired and yet relieved that the stress leading up to the funeral is over; it may even foster an atmosphere of reconciliation.

Usually the reception will not have a formal beginning, but if occasion presents itself, it may be good for someone to say a few words of welcome, appreciation, or prayer once everyone is present.

# Features of the Funeral Rites

---

An act of worship is made up of various elements, some of which are listed below. It helps to prepare the liturgy if you know something of the purpose of each part of it. Such knowledge will help to make sure that everything is given its proper importance, and the liturgy is arranged so that it is a true Christian celebration, and also that it allows everyone to take an active part.

## The Word of God

### Readings

The Word of God is of great importance in the funeral rite. The readings proclaim the meaning that Christ himself gave to death, teach us to remember the dead, nourish our hope of being gathered together again in God's kingdom, and encourage us to live the Christian life. Above all, the readings tell of God's designs for a world in which suffering and death will be destroyed. In the readings all present have an opportunity to hear God speak to them in their needs, sorrows, fears, and hopes.

At the funeral liturgy the biblical readings may not be replaced by non-biblical ones. But during prayer services with the family non-biblical readings may be used in addition to readings from Scripture (see below).

Members of the family may be invited to read the scripture readings.

Many people nowadays wish to include in the funeral a reading or poem which is not from the bible. Please bear the following points in mind.

In the celebration of the word of God at the funeral liturgy, the biblical readings may not be replaced. However, an additional reading, inspired by faith, could be appropriate as a meditation after the homily. Alternatively, a non-biblical reading may be incorporated into the words of remembrance spoken by a member of the family or a friend later in the funeral liturgy.

In a service at home or in hospital, non-biblical readings or poems can be used effectively, as these services are less formal than the funeral liturgy in church, though the Scriptures should not be entirely displaced.

---

## Psalms

The psalms express the suffering and pain, the hope and trust of people of every age. Above all they sing of faith in God and of redemption. They enable us to pray in the words that Jesus himself, who knew anguish and the fear of death, used during his life on earth.

Psalms are used in many places in the funeral rites, in particular as responses to the readings, and at the vigil service.

The psalms are songs, and should be sung whenever possible.

## Homily

A homily is always given after the gospel reading at the funeral liturgy and may also be given after the readings at the vigil service. It should be based on the readings and not be simply a talk in praise of the deceased person. Attentive to the grief of the people present, the preacher should dwell on God's compassionate love and on the death and resurrection of the Lord, showing how these were present in the life and death of the deceased and are active in their own lives too. Through the preacher's words, members of the family and community should receive consolation and strength to face the death of one of their members. The minister will also want to speak about the life of the dead person, and the consolation and hope the homily can offer will be enhanced if you and the minister can discuss this beforehand.

In addition a member of the family or a friend may wish to say a few words in remembrance of the deceased person. This is certainly possible at the vigil, whether this is held at home or in church. It is also possible at the funeral liturgy, whether this is a Mass or not. These words in remembrance are spoken towards the end of the vigil or funeral liturgy as you can see from the checklists on pages 19 and 21. You should discuss this option with the minister beforehand.

## Prayers and Intercessions

In the prayers of the funeral rites the presiding minister addresses God on behalf of the deceased and the mourners in the name of the whole Church. The minister and the family should aim to select texts that express the unspoken prayers and hopes of everyone present.

Having heard the Word of God, the assembly responds at the vigil and at the funeral liturgy with prayers of intercession for the deceased and all the dead, for the family and all who mourn, and for all present.

# Music

Music is part of the very structure of the funeral rites. It allows people to express feelings that words alone cannot convey. It has the power to console and uplift, and to strengthen the unity of the assembly in faith and love. The texts of the songs chosen should express the paschal mystery of the Lord's suffering, death, and triumph over death and should be related to the readings.  The music at funerals should help to create a spirit of hope in Christ's victory over death and in the Christian's share in that victory

There should be music for all parts of the funeral liturgy, whenever possible. When preparing the funeral, the priest or other person helping the family should be able to put them in touch with an organist and other musicians.

If you are thinking of including a piece of non-religious music, please ensure that it is in harmony with our faith in the Lord's death and resurrection and will contribute to the atmosphere of Christian worship.

# Silence

Silence is important in the celebration of the funeral rites. Intervals of silence should be observed, for example, after each reading and during the final commendation and farewell. This will give everyone time to reflect upon the word of God and the meaning of the celebration, and to allow expression to their thoughts, memories and prayers.

# Symbols

## Easter Candle and Other Candles

The Easter candle is a reminder of Christ's presence among us. It recalls the Easter Vigil, the night when the Church awaits the Lord's resurrection. During the funeral liturgy, and during the vigil service when celebrated in the church, the Easter candle may be placed beforehand near where the coffin will stand.

## Holy Water

Holy water is a reminder of the saving waters of baptism. In the rite of reception of the body at the church, it calls to mind the deceased's baptism and initiation into the community of faith. In the rite of final commendation the gesture of sprinkling may also signify farewell.

## Incense

Incense is used during the funeral rites as a sign of honour to the body of the deceased, which through baptism became the temple of the Holy Spirit. Incense is also used as a sign of the community's prayers for the deceased rising to the throne of God and as a sign of farewell.

## Other Symbols

If it is the custom in the local community, a pall (a large white cloth) may be placed over the coffin when it is received at the church. It is a reminder of the baptismal garment of the deceased and a sign of the Christian dignity of the person. It also signifies that all are equal in the eyes of God.

A Book of the Gospels or a Bible may be placed on the coffin as a sign that Christians live by the Word of God and that fidelity to that Word leads to eternal life.

A cross may be placed on the coffin as a reminder that the Christian is marked by the cross in baptism and through Jesus' suffering on the cross is brought to the victory of his resurrection.

Fresh flowers, in moderation, enhance the setting of the funeral rites.

Only Christian symbols may rest on or be placed near the coffin during the funeral liturgy.

## Liturgical Colour

The liturgical colour chosen for funerals should express Christian hope, but without being offensive to human grief.

White expresses the hope of Easter. Violet recalls the expectation of Advent and the Lenten preparation for Easter. Black is a token of mourning, but, in our society, is becoming much less associated with Christian hope.

# Movement

Processions, especially when accompanied with music and singing, can strengthen a sense of togetherness. During the various processions, it is preferable that the pallbearers carry the coffin as a sign of reverence and respect for the deceased. Family members or friends will be especially appropriate for this task. The mourners who follow the coffin may carry lighted candles which can be set down around the catafalque or the grave.

In most places a procession on foot to the church or to the place of committal may not be possible. Nevertheless at the conclusion of the funeral liturgy an antiphon and response may be sung as the body is borne down the church. Psalms, hymns, or liturgical songs may also be sung when people gather at the place of committal.

# Planning for the Crematorium

The time allocated at a crematorium will vary from place to place, but will always be sufficient for a committal following a service in church. However, when the funeral itself is to take place at the crematorium, you should consider the time available when choosing readings, hymns, and other elements for the service. It may be preferable to omit some options altogether, so that the remaining items can be used with dignity, reverence, and sensitivity to the occasion  Alternatively, you may wish to ask for a longer time than is usually provided. The most important thing is that the funeral be for you a dignified, reverent, and unhurried occasion.

# Checklists

The following pages provide a number of checklists which may be helpful when someone dies or when planning the funeral. For your convenience, these checklists may be freely photocopied.

On the liturgy planning sheets, items in square brackets [...] are optional. The complete texts of the Scripture readings and prayers are found in the pages following the checklists and each text is numbered.

A glance at these checklists will show just how many choices and options there are. However, you should not feel that you have to make all these decisions yourself. For instance, you may wish to choose scripture readings and music, but leave the choice of prayer texts to the parish clergy. You may make as many or as few choices as you like.

If you are using these notes to plan your own funeral, you will want to leave a copy of the completed checklists with your next of kin or executor, and perhaps also with your parish clergy.

# CHECKLIST 1: When someone dies

## Who will need to be informed as soon as possible?

- **the next of kin**, if not present
- **the family doctor**, if the person dies at home
- **the funeral director**, if the family is using one (the deceased may already have made arrangements)
- **the priest**

In addition, if you are called to someone who has died unexpectedly or in unusual circumstances, the police will need to be informed. Do not touch or move anything in the room.

## What happens next?

### Arranging the funeral

If the cause of death is clear, the doctor will issue a medical certificate and a formal notice confirming that he or she has signed the certificate. This notice gives information on how to register the death and will enable funeral arrangements to be made.

If the doctor reports the death to the coroner, there may be a delay while a post mortem or inquest is carried out. The coroner's office will advise you on what arrangements may be made.

### Registering the death

The death will need to be registered within five days unless it has been reported to the coroner. Further detail concerning these procedures can be found in a booklet available from the Department of Social Security.

## What are the financial implications?

If the family wishes to use a funeral director, it is quite proper to invite estimates from different firms.

There is a considerable financial difference between cremation and burial, and those choosing burial will also need to consider the upkeep of the grave.

There may be a fee for an organist or other musician.

An offering to the minister is discretionary, though customary, and you may wish to check. Where the family uses a funeral director an offering may be included automatically in the account, though the family is free to make its own arrangements.

# CHECKLIST 2: Planning the Liturgy

## FORM OF SERVICE

**Vigil** — page 4

Vigil? yes ☐ no ☐
if yes: where?
when?

**Reception of the Body into the Church** — page 6

simple form of reception ☐
at the vigil in church ☐
at the funeral liturgy ☐

**Funeral Liturgy** — page 8

funeral Mass in church ☐
or funeral service ☐
where?
when?

**Committal**

at the graveside ☐
at the crematorium ☐
elsewhere ☐
directly after funeral liturgy ☐
delayed? ☐ when?

**Ashes**

to be buried? yes ☐ no ☐
if yes: where?
when?

## ADDRESSES

| | |
|---|---|
| **Deceased** | |
| age | |
| **Next of kin** | |
| | |
| | |
| 'phone | |
| **Church** | |
| | |
| | |
| 'phone | |
| **Minister** | |
| | |
| 'phone | |
| fax | |
| **Funeral director** | |
| | |
| 'phone | |
| fax | |
| **Organist/musician** | |
| | |
| 'phone | |
| fax | |
| **Cemetery/crematorium** | |
| | |
| 'phone | |

# VIGIL FOR THE DECEASED

♪ indicates the music priorities

* indicates elements which take place when the body is received into church

[ ] indicates optional elements

## INTRODUCTORY RITES

Greeting

\* Sprinkling with Holy Water

\* Entrance Procession   \* bearers

♪   song / music

\* Placing of the Pall   yes ☐   no ☐
   if yes, by

\* Placing of   yes ☐   no ☐
Christian Symbols   which
   by

Opening Prayer   number

## LITURGY OF THE WORD

First Reading   no.   ref.
   reader
   subject

♪ Psalm   no.   ref.
   musician(s)
   response

Second Reading   no.   ref.
   reader
   subject

## LITURGY OF THE WORD continued

♪ Gospel   no.
Acclamation   setting   ref.

Gospel   no.
   reader
   subject

Homily   preacher

## PRAYER OF INTERCESSION

♪ Litany   said ☐ reader
   or sung ☐ music setting
   singer

♪ The Lord's Prayer   said ☐
   or sung ☐ music setting

Concluding Prayer   number

Words in
Remembrance   speaker

## CONCLUDING RITE

Blessing

♪ Conclusion   music ☐ silence ☐
   song

# FUNERAL LITURGY

&bull; indicates the music priorities

* indicates elements which take place when the body is received into church

[] indicates optional elements

## INTRODUCTORY RITES

| | | |
|---|---|---|
| | Greeting | |
| * | Sprinkling with Holy Water | |
| &bull; | Entrance Procession | * bearers |
| | | song / music |
| * | Placing of the Pall | yes ☐  no ☐ |
| | if yes, by | |
| * | Placing of Christian Symbols | yes ☐  no ☐ |
| | | which |
| | | by |
| | Opening Prayer | number |

## LITURGY OF THE WORD

| | | | |
|---|---|---|---|
| | First Reading | no. | ref. |
| | | reader | |
| | | subject | |
| &bull; | Psalm | no. | ref. |
| | | musician(s) | |
| | | response | |
| | Second Reading | no. | ref. |
| | | reader | |
| | | subject | |

## LITURGY OF THE WORD *continued*

| | | | |
|---|---|---|---|
| &bull; | Gospel Acclamation | no. | |
| | | setting | |
| | Gospel | no. | ref. |
| | | reader | |
| | | subject | |
| | Homily | preacher | |
| | General Intercessions | writer | |
| | | reader | |

WHEN MASS IS NOT CELEBRATED THE SERVICE CONTINUES WITH THE FINAL COMMENDATION OVERLEAF

## LITURGY OF THE EUCHARIST

| | | | |
|---|---|---|---|
| | Procession with the Gifts | by | |
| | | music ☐   silence ☐ | |
| | | song | |
| &bull; | Eucharistic Prayer | number | |
| | | music setting | |
| | The Lord's Prayer | said ☐ | |
| | | or  sung ☐  music setting | |
| | Breaking of Bread | music | |
| | Communion | ministers | |
| &bull; | processional song | | |
| | song of thanksgiving | | |
| | | or  silence ☐ | |

## FINAL COMMENDATION

[ Words in
Remembrance        speaker

[ Removal of
Christian Symbols    by

Invitation to prayer    number

🎼  Song of Farewell    number

                       music setting

Prayer of
Commendation    number

## PROCESSION TO THE PLACE OF COMMITTAL

🎼  Processional song

                       music

                       bearers

## RITE OF COMMITTAL

Prayer over the Place
of Committal (burial)    number

Prayer before Committal
(cremation)    number

Committal    number

Intercessions    reader

Concluding Prayer    number

Leave-taking gesture    yes ☐  no ☐

                       if yes:    which

# Some Music Suggestions

Most of us are rarely asked to choose music for a church service and may not know where to start. This list is provided to give some ideas. (It is not an 'official list' of approved music.)

Sometimes there is already a starting point: the wishes of the dead person. These may have been written down, or you may know a favourite hymn or hymns which they would have wanted or which you yourself find inspiring or comforting. This list cannot include every possible hymn, but it contains some which have been found helpful and may help you think of others.

Much new music has been written in recent years. If you see a title here which you would like to know more about, the organist or whoever will be leading the music may be able to help you.

If you find the task of choosing music daunting, please say so. In the same way you may not feel like singing, but there will be other people at the funeral who will sing for you.

## Traditional Hymns*

Abide with me
All my hope on God is founded
Be thou my vision
Firmly I believe and truly
For all the saints
Guide me, O thou great redeemer
I heard the voice of Jesus say
O Jesus, I have promised
Lead, kindly light
Lord of all hopefulness
Now the green blade riseth
O God, our help in ages past
Praise to the holiest in the height
Praise we our God with joy
Sing with all the saints in glory
Soul of my Saviour
Thine be the glory

## Modern Hymns and Songs*

Be still and know I am with you
Be not afraid
Go, silent friend
How great thou art
I am the bread of life
Like a child rests
Jesu, son of Mary
O the love of my Lord
On eagle's wings
There is a longing in our hearts
Unless a grain of wheat
We walk by faith
Yahweh, I know you are near

## Taizé chants

Bless the Lord, my soul
Jesus, remember me
O Lord, hear my prayer
O Christe, Domine Jesu
In the Lord I'll be ever thankful

*You may also find suitable hymns in the following categories in the hymnbook used in the parish: Anointing and Healing, Comfort, Eternal Life, Faith, Guidance, Hope and Trust, Love of God for us, Peace, Praise, Funerals, Easter

## Latin Requiem Mass

Some parts of this (*In paradisum, Requiem Aeternam, Sanctus* and *Agnus Dei*) are to be found in *Music for the Funeral Rite* (MFR, McCrimmon 1990) and *Laudate* (Decani Music, 1999.)

## Psalms

To have a Responsorial Psalm sung, as in many places on Sundays, a singer will be needed. They will be able to find a setting of most of the psalms printed on pp. 34-37 below in the book they use for Sundays, or in *Music for the Funeral Rite.*

 Some other modern psalm settings are:
* *Psalm 22(23)*: Because the Lord is my shepherd (Walker) *or*
            Shepherd me, O God (Haugen) - requires a singer
* *Psalm 41(42)*: As the deer longs (Hurd) *or*
            O God. for you I long (Farrell)
* *Psalm 62(63)*: Your love is finer than life (Haugen) - requires a singer

If there is no singer available, the psalm may be sung by everybody present as a hymn or song:
* *Psalm 22(23)*: The Lord's my shepherd *or*
            The king of love my shepherd is
* *Psalm 102(103)*: Praise, my soul, the King of heaven
* *Psalm 41(42)*:  As longs the deer

## Alleluia

The Gospel Acclamation is important as it prepares everyone to listen to the Gospel.  Most people will know the Easter (or Paschal) alleluia and if there is someone to start it off, the organist or the priest, will join in.  In Lent the Gospel Acclamation is not Alleluia but 'Praise to you O Christ, King of eternal glory' or a similar verse.

## Mass Settings

If at all possible *the Holy, Holy, Memorial Acclamation* and *Great Amen* should be sung at Mass. You will know if there is some music which is familiar in the parish and likely to be easy for the people attending to sing.

## Songs of Farewell (see p.76 below)

May the choirs of angels
Saints of God (MFR, nos. 21 & 44)
I know that my redeemer lives (MFR, *Laudate*)

## Procession from Church  (see p.79 below)

May flights of angels (MFR)
May God the Father look on you (*Laudate*)
May the angels lead you into paradise (MFR)
May choirs of angels welcome you (MFR)

# Useful Addresses

## Catholic AIDS Preventative Support (CAPS)

*provides support for people with HIV or AIDS, their partners, families, friends, and carers*

Martin Pendergast,
P O Box 24632, London E9 6XF
Tel No: 020 8986 0807
Email: martin@lymegrove.clara.co.uk

## Citizens' Advice Bureaux

*provide practical assistance and advice, especially where there are legal or finance problems*
See local telephone directory or use website to identify local branches
www.citizensadvice.org.uk

## Compassionate Friends

*provide help for bereaved parents*
53 North Street, Bristol BS3 1EN
Helpline 08451 232304 (offer local support and send leaflets - manned 7 days a week 10-4, 6.30-10.30)
Email: info@tcf.org.uk
www.tcf.org.uk

## Cruse Bereavement Care

*provides help for anyone who has been bereaved; send S.A.E. for information*
Helpline: 0870 167 1677
email: helpline@crusebereavementcare.org.uk
www.crusebereavementcare.org.uk

## Department of Social Security

*provides advice on benefits which may be available*
See local telephone directory or use website to identify local branches
http://www.dwp.gov.uk/

## The Foundation for the Study of Infant Deaths

*provides help for those bereaved by a cot death*
24 hour helpline: 020 7233 2090
email: fsid@sids.org.uk
www.sids.org.uk

## Miscarriage Association

*provides information and support for women who have suffered a miscarriage or ectopic pregnancy. It has a network of local contacts around the UK with whom women can share their feelings.*
helpline 01924 200799
www.miscarriageassociation.org.uk

## The Natural Death Centre

6 Blackstock Mews, Blackstock Road, London N4 2BT
Tel: 0871 288 2098  Fax: 020 7354 3831
www.naturaldeath.org. uk

## National Association of Widows

*provides an information service and local social groups*
48 Queens Road, Coventry, CV1 3EH
024 7663 4848 (answerphone at times)
www.widows.uk.net or www.nawidows.org.uk

## Samaritans

*provide support for anyone in need*
Telephone calls to the national number (08457 909090) are charged at the local rate.
Details of local branch can be obtained from that number or the website
Email: jo@samaritans.org
www. samaritans.org.uk

## The Stillbirth and Neonatal Death Society (SANDS)

*provides help for parents bereaved by a still birth or neonatal death*
SANDS, 28 Portland Place, London W1B 1LY
Tel: 020 7436 5881
Helpline open 9.30-5.30 Mon-Fri
General enquiries 020 7436 7940
Fax: 020 7436 3715
Email: helpline@uk-sands.org
www.uk-sands.org

## Support after Murder and Manslaughter

*provides help and support for those bereaved through tragic death*
Cramer House, 39 Brixton Road, London SW9 6DZ
Tel: 020 7735 3838 Fax: 020 7735 3900
www.samm.org.uk

# Scripture readings

# Readings from the Old Testament

1     *A reading from the book of Job (19:1.23-27)*

       *This I know: that my Avenger lives*

Job said:

      'Ah, would that these words of mine were written down,
    inscribed on some monument with iron chisel and engraving tool,
    cut into the rock for ever.
      This I know: that my Avenger lives,
    and he, the Last, will take his stand on earth.
    After my awaking, he will set me close to him,
    and from my flesh I shall look on God.
    He whom I shall see will take my part:
    these eyes will gaze on him and find him not aloof.'

      *This is the word of the Lord.*

*Psalm 26 is suggested to follow this reading, see p 35*

    ℞.     The Lord is my light and my help.
    *or*
    ℞.     I am sure I shall see the Lord's goodness
           in the land of the living.


2     *A reading from the book of Wisdom (3:1-9)*

      *He accepted them as a holocaust.*

The souls of the virtuous are in the hands of God,
no torment shall ever touch them.
In the eyes of the unwise, they did appear to die,
their going looked like a disaster,
their leaving us, like annihilation;
but they are in peace.
If they experienced punishment as men see it,
their hope was rich with immortality;
slight was their affliction, great will their blessings be.
God has put them to the test
and proved them worthy to be with him;
he has tested them like gold in a furnace,
and accepted them as a holocaust.
When the time comes for his visitation they will shine out;
as sparks run through the stubble, so will they.
They shall judge nations, rule over peoples,
and the Lord will be their king for ever.
They who trust in him will understand the truth,

those who are faithful will live with him in love;
for grace and mercy await those he has chosen.

*This is the word of the Lord.*

---

SHORTER FORM

## A reading from the book of Wisdom        (3:1-6 9)

*He accepted them as a holocaust.*
The souls of the virtuous are in the hands of God,
no torment shall ever touch them.
In the eyes of the unwise, they did appear to die,
their going looked like a disaster,
their leaving us, like annihilation;
but they are in peace.
If they experienced punishment as men see it,
their hope was rich with immortality;
slight was their affliction, great will their blessing be.
God has put them to the test
and proved them worthy to be with him;
he has tested them like gold in a furnace,
and accepted them as a holocaust.
They who trust in him will understand the truth,
those who are faithful will live with him in love;
for grace and mercy await those he has chosen.

*This is the word of the Lord.*

---

*Psalm 114 (115) is suggested to follow this reading, see p.36*
        ℞. I will walk in the presence of the Lord
            in the land of the living.

## 3 A reading from the book of Wisdom  (4:7-15)

*Untarnished life, this is ripe old age.*
The virtuous man, though he die before his time, will find rest.
Length of days is not what makes age honourable,
nor number of years the true measure of life;
understanding, this is man's grey hairs,
untarnished life, this is ripe old age.
    He has sought to please God,
so God has loved him;
as he was living among sinners, he has been taken up.
He has been carried off so that evil may not warp his understanding

or treachery seduce his soul;
for the fascination of evil throws good things into the shade,
and the whirlwind of desire corrupts a simple heart.
Coming to perfection in so short a while, he achieved long life;
his soul being pleasing to the Lord,
he has taken him quickly from the wickedness around him.
Yet people look on, uncomprehending;
it does not enter their heads
that grace and mercy await the chosen of the Lord,
and protection, his holy ones.

> *This is the word of the Lord.*

*Psalm 22 is suggested to follow this reading, see p.34*
> ℟. If I should walk in the valley of darkness
>     no evil would I fear,
>       for you are there with me.

*Psalm 22 is suggested to follow this reading, see p.34*

4      **A reading from the prophet Isaiah**   (25:6-9)

> *The Lord will destroy Death for ever.*
On this mountain,
the Lord of hosts will prepare for all peoples
a banquet of rich food.
   On this mountain he will remove
the mourning veil covering all peoples,
and the shroud enwrapping all nations,
he will destroy Death for ever.
The Lord will wipe away
the tears from every cheek;
he will take away his people's shame
everywhere on earth,
for the Lord has said so.
That day, it will be said: See, this is our God
in whom we hoped for salvation;
the Lord is the one in whom we hoped.
We exult and we rejoice that he has saved us.

> *This is the word of the Lord.*

*Psalm 22 is suggested to follow this reading, see p.34*
> ℟. The Lord is my shepherd;
>     there is nothing I shall want.

5        *A reading from the book of Lamentations*          *(3:17-26)*

*It is good to wait in silence for the Lord to save.*

My soul is shut out from peace;
I have forgotten happiness.
And now I say,'My strength is gone,
that hope which came from the Lord'.
Brooding on my anguish and affliction
is gall and wormwood.
My spirit ponders it continually
and sinks within me.
This is what I shall tell my heart,
and so recover hope:
the favours of the Lord are not all past,
his kindnesses are not exhausted;
every morning they are renewed;
great is his faithfulness.
'My portion is the Lord' says my soul
'and so I will hope in him.'
The Lord is good to those who trust him,
to the soul that searches for him.
It is good to wait in silence
for the Lord to save.

*This is the word of the Lord.*

*Psalm 24 is suggested to follow this reading, see p.34*          *or*
   ℟.  To you, O Lord, I lift up my soul.          ℟.  Those who hope in you, O Lord,
                                           shall not be disappointed.

6        *A reading from the prophet Daniel (12:1-3)*

*Those who lie sleeping in the dust will awake.*

I , Daniel, was doing penance when I received this message from the Lord:
'At that time Michael will stand up, the great prince who mounts guard over your people. There is going to be a time of great distress, unparalleled since nations first came into existence. When that time comes, your own people will be spared, all those whose names are found written in the Book. Of those who lie sleeping in the dust of the earth many will awake, some to everlasting life, some to shame and everlasting disgrace. The learned will shine as brightly as the vault of heaven, and those who have instructed many in virtue, as bright as stars for all eternity.'

*This is the word of the Lord.*

*Psalm 41 is suggested to follow this reading, see p.35*
   ℟.  My soul is thirsting for God,
      the God of my life.

7      *A reading from the second book of Maccabees (12:43-45)*

> *A fine and noble action, in which he took account of the resurrection.*

Judas, the leader of the Jews, took a collection from the people individually, amounting to nearly two thousand drachmae, and sent it to Jerusalem to have a sacrifice for sin offered, an altogether fine and noble action, in which he took full account of the resurrection. For if he had not expected the fallen to rise again it would have been superfluous and foolish to pray for the dead, whereas if he had in view the splendid recompense reserved for those who make a pious end, the thought was holy and devout. This was why he had this atonement sacrifice offered for the dead, so that they might be released from their sin.

> *This is the word of the Lord.*

*Psalm 102 is suggested to follow this reading, see p.36*

> ℟. The Lord is compassion and love.

*or*

> ℟. The salvation of the just
> comes from the Lord.

# First Readings from the New Testament

for Eastertide

1    ## A reading from the Acts of the Apostles (10:34-43)

*God has appointed Jesus to judge everyone, alive or dead.*

Peter addressed Cornelius and his household:

'The truth I have now come to realise,' he said, 'is that God does not have favourites, but that anybody of any nationality who fears God and does what is right is acceptable to him.

'It is true, God sent his word to the people of Israel, and it was to them that the good news of peace was brought by Jesus Christ - but Jesus Christ is Lord of all men. You must have heard about the recent happenings in Judaea; about Jesus of Nazareth and how he began in Galilee, after John had been preaching baptism. God had anointed him with the Holy Spirit and with power, and because God was with him, Jesus went about doing good and curing all who had fallen into the power of the devil. Now I, and those with me, can witness to everything he did throughout the countryside of Judaea and in Jerusalem itself: and also to the fact that they killed him by hanging him on a tree, yet three days afterwards God raised him to life and allowed him to be seen, not by the whole people but only by certain witnesses God had chosen beforehand. Now we are those witnesses we have eaten and drunk with him after his resurrection from the dead - and he has ordered us to proclaim this to his people and to tell them that God has appointed him to judge everyone alive or dead. It is to him that all the prophets bear this witness: that all who believe in Jesus will have their sins forgiven through his name.

*This is the word of the Lord.*

---

SHORTER FORM

## A reading from the Acts of the Apostles (10:34-36. 42-43)

*God has appointed Jesus to judge everyone, alive or dead.*

Peter addressed Cornelius and his household:

'The truth I have now come to realise,' he said, 'is that God does not have favourites, but that anybody of any nationality who fears God and does what is right is acceptable to him.

'It is true, God sent his word to the people of Israel, and it was to them that the good news of peace was brought by Jesus Christ - but Jesus Christ is Lord of all men, and he has ordered us to proclaim this to his people and to tell them that God has appointed him to judge everyone alive or dead. It is to him that all the prophets bear this witness: that all who believe in Jesus will have their sins forgiven through his name.

*This is the word of the Lord.*

---

*Psalm 62 is suggested to follow this reading, see p.35*

℞. For you my soul is thirsting,
O Lord, my God.

**2**      **A reading from the book of the Apocalypse**      **(14:13)**

*Happy are those who die in the Lord!*

I, John, heard a voice from heaven say to me, 'Write down: Happy are those who die in the Lord!
Happy indeed, the Spirit says; now they can rest for ever after their work, since their good deeds go with them.'

*This is the word of the Lord.*

*Psalm 129 is suggested to follow this reading, see p.37*

℞. Out of the depths, I cry to you, O Lord.
*or*
℞. I wait for the Lord,
I count on his word.

**3**      **A reading from the book of the Apocalypse (20:11-21:1)**

*The dead were judged according to what they had done in their lives.*

I, John, saw a great white throne and the One who was sitting on it. In his presence, earth and sky vanished, leaving no trace. I saw the dead, both great and small, standing in front of his throne, while the book of life was opened, and other books opened which were the record of what they had done in their lives, by which the dead were judged.

The sea gave up all the dead who were in it; Death and Hades were emptied of the dead that were in them; and every one was judged according to the way in which he had lived. Then Death and Hades were thrown into the burning lake. This burning lake is the second death; and anybody whose name could not be found written in the book of life was thrown into the burning lake.

Then I saw a new heaven and a new earth; the first heaven and the first earth had disappeared now, and there was no longer any sea.

*This is the word of the Lord.*

*Psalm 142 is suggested to follow this reading, see p.37*

℞. Lord, listen to my prayer.

4    *A reading from the book of the Apocalypse* (1:1-7)

*There will be no more death*

I, John, saw a new heaven and a new earth; the first heaven and the first earth had disappeared now, and there was no longer any sea. I saw the holy city, and the new Jerusalem, coming down from God out of heaven, as beautiful as a bride all dressed for her husband. Then I heard a loud voice call from the throne, 'You see this city? Here God lives among men. He will make his home among them; they shall be his people, and he will be their God; his name is God-with-them. He will wipe away all tears from their eyes; there will be no more death, and no more mourning or sadness. The world of the past has gone.'

Then the One sitting on the throne spoke 'Now I am making the whole of creation new,' he said. 'I will give water from the well of life free to anybody who is thirsty; it is the rightful inheritance of the one who proves victorious; and I will be his God and he a son to me.

*This is the word of the Lord.*

*Psalm 121 is suggested to follow this reading, see p.36*

*Psalm 121 is suggested to follow this reading, see p.36*

    ℞. I rejoiced when I heard them say:
      'Let us go to God's house.'
       *or*
    ℞. Let us go to God's house, rejoicing.

# Responsorial Psalms

**1    Psalm 22**

**The Lord is my shepherd;
there is nothing I shall want.**
*or*
**If I should walk in the valley of  darkness
no evil would I fear,
for you are there with me.**


The Lord is my shepherd;
there is nothing I shall want.
Fresh and green are the pastures
where he gives me repose.
Near restful waters he leads me,
to revive my drooping spirit.

He guides me along the right path;
he is true to his name.
If I should walk in the valley of darkness
no evil would I fear.
You are there with your crook and your staff;
with these you give me comfort.

You have prepared a banquet for me
in the sight of my foes.
My head you have anointed with oil;
my cup is overflowing.

Surely goodness and kindness shall follow me
all the days of my life.
In the Lord's own house shall I dwell
for ever and ever.


**2    Psalm 24    (6-7. 17-18. 20-21)**

**To you, O Lord, I lift up my soul.**
*or*
**Those who hope in you, O Lord,
shall not be disappointed.**

Remember your mercy, Lord,
and the love you have shown from of old.
In your love remember me,
because of your goodness, O Lord.

Relieve the anguish of my heart
and set me free from my distress.
See my affliction and my toil
and take all my sins away.

Preserve my life and rescue me.
Do not disappoint me, you are my refuge.
May innocence and uprightness protect me:
for my hope is in you, O Lord.

34

3       **Psalm 26**       (1. 4. 7-9. 13-14)

**The Lord is my light and my help.**

*or*

**I am sure I shall see the Lord's goodness
in the land of the living.**

The Lord is my light and my help;
whom shall I fear?
The Lord is the stronghold of my life;
before whom shall I shrink?

There is one thing I ask of the Lord,
for this I long,
to live in the house of the Lord,
all the days of my life,
to savour the sweetness of the Lord,
to behold his temple.

O Lord, hear my voice when I call;
have mercy and answer.
It is your face, O Lord, that I seek;
hide not your face.

I am sure I shall see the Lord's goodness
in the land of the living.
Hope in him, hold firm and take heart.
Hope in the Lord!

3       **Psalm 41**       (2.3.5)

**My soul is thirsting for God,
the God of my life.**

Like the deer that yearns
for running streams,
so my soul is yearning
for you, my God.

My soul is thirsting for God,
the God of my life;
when can I enter and see
the face of God?

These things will I remember
as I pour out my soul:
how I would lead the rejoicing crowd
into the house of God,
amid cries of gladness and thanksgiving
the throng wild with joy.

4       **Psalm 62**       (2-6. 8-9)

**For you my soul is thirsting,
O Lord, my God.**

O God, you are my God, for you I long;
for you my soul is thirsting.
My body pines for you
like a dry, weary land without water.

So I gaze on you in the sanctuary
to see your strength and your glory.
For your love is better than life,
my lips will speak your praise.

So I will bless you all my life,
in your name I will lift up my hands.
My soul shall be filled as with a banquet,
my mouth shall praise you with joy.

You have been my help;
in the shadow of your wings I rejoice.
My soul clings to you;
your right hand holds me fast.

5      *Psalm 102*        *(8.10. 13-18)*

**The Lord is compassion and love.**
*or*
**The salvation of the just
comes from the Lord.**

The Lord is compassion and love,
slow to anger and rich in mercy.
He does not treat us according to our sins
nor repay us according to our faults.

As a father has compassion on his sons,
the Lord has pity on those who fear him;
for he knows of what we are made,
he remembers that we are dust.

As for man, his days are like grass;
he flowers like the flower of the field;
the wind blows and he is gone
and his place never sees him again.

But the love of the Lord is everlasting
upon those who hold him in fear;
his justice reaches out to children's children
when they keep his covenant in truth.

6      *Psalms 114 & 115*      *(114:5-8;
115:10-11. 15-16)*

**I will walk in the presence of the Lord
in the land of the living.**
*or*
**Alleluia!**

How gracious is the Lord, and just;
our God has compassion.
The Lord protects the simple hearts;
I was helpless so he saved me.

I trusted, even when I said:
'I am sorely afflicted,'
and when I said in my alarm:
'No man can be trusted'.

O precious in the eyes of the Lord
is the death of his faithful.
Your servant, Lord, your servant am I;
you have loosened my bonds.

7      *Psalm 121*

**I rejoiced when I heard them say:
let us go to God's house.'**
*or*
**Let us go to God's house, rejoicing.**

I rejoiced when I heard them say:
'Let us go to God's house.'
And now our feet are standing
within your gates, O Jerusalem.

Jerusalem is built as a city
strongly compact.
It is there that the tribes go up,
the tribes of the Lord.

For Israel's law it is,
there to praise the Lord's name.
There were set the thrones of judgement
of the house of David.

For the peace of Jerusalem pray:
'Peace be to your homes!
May peace reign in your walls,
in your palaces, peace!'

For love of my brethren and friends
I say: 'Peace upon you!'
For love of the house of the Lord
I will ask for your good.

8       *Psalm 129*

**Out of the depths I cry to you, O Lord.**
*or*
**I wait for the Lord,**
**I count on his word.**

Out of the depths I cry to you, O Lord,
Lord, hear my voice!
O let your ears be attentive
to the voice of my pleading.

If you, O Lord, should mark our guilt.
Lord, who would survive?
But with you is found forgiveness,
for this we revere you.

My soul is waiting for the Lord,
I count on his word.
My soul is longing for the Lord
more than watchman for daybreak.

Because with the Lord there is mercy
and fullness of redemption.
Israel indeed he will redeem
from all its iniquity.

9       *Psalm 142*                                        *(1-2. 5-8. 10)*

**Lord, listen to my prayer.**

Lord, listen to my prayer:
turn your ear to my appeal.
You are faithful, you are just; give answer.
Do not call your servant to judgement
for no one is just in your sight.

I remember the days that are past:
I ponder. all your works.
I muse on what your hand has wrought
and to you I stretch out my hands.
Like a parched land my soul thirsts for you.

Lord, make haste and give me answer;
for my spirit fails within me.
In the morning let me know your love
for I put my trust in you.

Teach me to do your will
for you, O Lord, are my God.
Let your good spirit guide me
in ways that are level and smooth.

# New Testament Second Readings

1      **A reading from the letter of St Paul to the Romans**      (5:5-11)

*Having died to make us righteous, is it likely that he would now fail to save us from God's anger?*
Hope is not deceptive, because the love of God has been poured into our hearts by the Holy Spirit which has been given us. We were still helpless when at his appointed moment Christ died for sinful men. It is not easy to die even for a good man - though of course for someone really worthy, a man might be prepared to die - but what proves that God loves us is that Christ died for us while we were still sinners. Having died to make us righteous, is it likely that he would now fail to save us from God's anger? When we were reconciled to God by the death of his Son, we were still enemies; now that we have been reconciled, surely we may count on being saved by the life of his Son? Not merely because we have been reconciled but because we are filled with joyful trust in God, through our Lord Jesus Christ, through whom we have already gained our reconciliation.

*This is the word of the Lord.*

2      **A reading from the letter of St Paul to the Romans**      s(5:17-21)

*However great the number of sins committed, grace was even greater.*
If it is certain that death reigned over everyone as the consequence of one man's    fall, it is even more certain that one man, Jesus Christ, will cause everyone to reign in life who receives the free gift that he does not deserve, of being made righteous. Again, as one man's fall brought condemnation on everyone, so the good act of one man brings everyone life and makes them justified. As by one man's disobedience many were made sinners, so by one man's obedience many will be made righteous. When law came, it was to multiply the opportunities of falling, but however great the number of sins committed, grace was even greater; and so, just as sin reigned wherever there was death, so grace will reign to bring eternal life thanks to the righteousness that comes through Jesus Christ our Lord.

*This is the word of the Lord.*

3      **A reading from the letter of St Paul to the Romans**      (6:3-9)

*Let us live a new life.*
When we were baptised in Christ Jesus we were baptised in his death; in other words, when we were baptised we went into the tomb with him and joined him in death, so that as Christ was raised from the dead by the Father's glory, we too might live a new

life. If in union with Christ we have imitated his death, we shall also imitate him in his resurrection. We must realise that our former selves have been crucified with him to destroy this sinful body and to free us from the slavery of sin. When a man dies, of course, he has finished with sin.

But we believe that having died with Christ we shall return to life with him: Christ, as we know, having been raised from the dead will never die again. Death has no power over him any more.

*This is the word of the Lord.*

---

SHORTER FORM

### A reading from the letter of St Paul to the Romans          (6:3-4. 8-9)

*Let us live a new life.*

When we were baptised in Christ Jesus we were baptised in his death; in other words, when we were baptised we went into the tomb with him and joined him in death, so that as Christ was raised from the dead by the Father's glory, we too might live a new life.

But we believe that having died with Christ we shall return to life with him: Christ, as we know, having been raised from the dead will never die again. Death has no power over him any more.

*This is the word of the Lord.*

---

4     ### A reading from the letter of St Paul to the Romans  (8:14-23)

*We wait for our bodies to be set free.*

Everyone moved by the Spirit is a son of God. The spirit you received is not the spirit of slaves bringing fear into your lives again; it is the spirit of sons, and it makes us cry out, 'Abba, Father!' The Spirit himself and our spirit bear united witness that we are children of God. And if we are children we are heirs as well: heirs of God and coheirs with Christ, sharing his sufferings so as to share his glory.

I think that what we suffer in this life can never be compared to the glory, as yet unrevealed, which is waiting for us. The whole creation is eagerly waiting for God to reveal his sons. It was not for any fault on the part of creation that it was made unable to attain its purpose, it was made so by God; but creation still retains the hope of being freed, like us, from its: slavery to decadence, to enjoy the same freedom and glory as the children of God. From the beginning till now the entire creation, as we know, has been groaning in one great act of giving birth; and not only creation, but all of us who possess the first-fruits of the Spirit, we too groan inwardly as we wait for our bodies to be set free.

*This is the word of the Lord.*

5          *A reading from the letter of St Paul to the Romans*          (8:31-35. 37-39)

*Nothing can come between us and the love of Christ.*

With God on our side who can be against us? Since God did not spare his own Son, but gave him up to benefit us all, we may be certain, after such a gift, that he will not refuse anything he can give. Could anyone accuse those that God has chosen? When God acquits, could anyone condemn? Could Christ Jesus? No! He not only died for us - he rose from the dead, and there at God's right hand he stands and pleads for us.

Nothing therefore can come between us and the love of Christ, even if we are troubled or worried, or being persecuted, or lacking food or clothes, or being threatened or even attacked. These are the trials through which we triumph, by the power of him who loved us. For I am certain of this: neither death nor life, no angel, no prince, nothing that exists, nothing still to come, not any power, or height or depth, nor any created thing, can ever come between us and the love of God made visible in Christ Jesus our Lord.

*This is the word of the Lord.*

6          *A reading from the letter of St Paul to the Romans*          (14:7-12)

*Alive or dead, we belong to the Lord*

The life and death of each of us has its influence on others; if we live, we live for the Lord; and if we die, we die for the Lord, so that alive or dead we belong to the Lord. This explains why Christ both died and came to life, it was so that he might be Lord both of the dead and of the living. We shall all have to stand before the judgement seat of God; as scripture says: By my life - it is the Lord who speaks - every knee shall bend before me, and every tongue shall praise God. It is to God, therefore, that each of us must give an account of himself.

*This is the word of the Lord.*

7          *A reading from the first letter of St Paul to the Corinthians* (15:20-23)

*All will be brought to life in Christ.*

Christ has been raised from the dead, the first-fruits of all who have fallen asleep. Death came through one man and in the same way the resurrection of the dead has come through one man. Just as all men die in Adam, so all men will be brought to life in Christ; but all of them in their proper order; Christ as the first-fruits and then, after the coming of Christ, those who belong to him. After that will come the end, when he hands over the kingdom to God the Father. For he must be king until he has put all his enemies under his feet and the last of the enemies to be destroyed is death, for everything is to be put under his feet. – Though when it is said that everything is subjected, this clearly cannot include the One who subjected everything to him. And when everything is subjected to him, then the Son himself will be subject in his turn to the One who subjected all things to him, so that God may be all in all.

*This is the word of the Lord.*

### A reading from the first letter of St Paul to the Corinthians (15:20-23)

*All men will be brought to life in Christ.*

Christ has been raised from the dead, the first-fruits of all who have fallen asleep. Death came through one man and in the same way the resurrection of the dead has come through one man. Just as all men die in Adam, so all men will be brought to life in Christ; but all of them in their proper order: Christ as the first-fruits and then, after the coming of Christ, those who belong to him,

*This is the word of the Lord.*

---

8    ### A reading from the first letter of St Paul to the Corinthians      (15:51-57)

*Death is swallowed up in victory.*

I will tell you something that has been secret: that we are not all going to die, but we shall all be changed. This will be instantaneous, in the twinkling of an eye, when the last trumpet sounds. It will sound, and the dead will be raised, imperishable, and we shall be changed as well, because our present perishable nature must put on imperishability and this mortal nature must put on immortality. When this perishable nature has put on imperishability, and when this mortal nature has put on immortality, then the words of scripture will come true: Death is swallowed up in victory. Death, where is your victory? Death, where is your sting? Now the sting of death is sin, and sin gets its power from the Law. So let us thank God for giving us the victory through our Lord Jesus Christ.

*This is the word of the Lord.*

---

9    ### A reading from the second letter of St Paul to the Corinthians      (4:14-5:1)

*Visible things last only for a time, but the invisible are eternal.*

We know that he who raised the Lord Jesus to life will raise us with Jesus in     our turn, and put us by his side and you with us. You see, all this is for your benefit, so that the more grace is multiplied among people, the more thanksgiving there will be, to the glory of God. That is why there is no weakening on our part, and instead, though this outer man of ours may be falling into decay, the inner man is renewed day by day. Yes, the troubles which are soon over, though they weigh little, train us for the carrying of a weight of eternal glory which is out of all proportion to them. And so we have no eyes for things that are visible, but only for things that are invisible; for visible things last only for a time, and the invisible things are eternal.

For we know that when the tent that we live in on earth is folded up, there is a house built by God for us, an everlasting home not made by human hands, in the heavens.

*This is the word of the Lord.*

10      *A reading from the second letter of St Paul to the Corinthians*      (5:1. 6-10)

*We have an everlasting home in the heavens.*

We know that when the tent that we live in on earth is folded up, there is a house built by God for us, an everlasting home not made by human hands, in the heavens.

We are always full of confidence, then, when we remember that to live in the body means to be exiled from the Lord, going as we do by faith and not by sight - we are full of confidence, I say, and actually want to be exiled from the body and make our home with the Lord. Whether we are living in the body or exiled from it, we are intent on pleasing him. For all the truth about us will be brought out in the law court of Christ, and each of us will get what he deserves for the things he did in the body, good or bad.

*This is the word of the Lord.*


11      *A reading from the letter of St Paul to the Philippians*      (3:20-21)

*He will transform these wretched bodies of ours into copies of his glorious body*

For us, our homeland is in heaven, and from heaven comes the saviour we are     waiting for, the Lord Jesus Christ, and he will transfigure these wretched bodies of ours into copies of his glorious body. He will do that by the same power with which he can subdue the whole universe.

*This is the word of the Lord.*


12      *A reading from the first letter of St Paul to the Thessalonians*      (4:13-18)

*We shall stay with the Lord for ever.*

We want you to be quite certain, brothers, about those who have died, to make sure that you do not grieve about them, like the other people who have no hope. We believe that Jesus died and rose again, and that it will be the same for those who have died in Jesus: God will bring them with him. We can tell you this from the Lord's own teaching, that any of us who are left alive until the Lord's coming will not have any advantage over those who have died. At the trumpet of God, the voice of the archangel will call out the command and the Lord himself will come down from heaven; those who have died in Christ will be the first to rise, and then those of us who are still alive will be taken up in the clouds, together with them, to meet the Lord in the air. So we shall stay with the Lord for ever. With such thoughts as these you should comfort one another.

*This is the word of the Lord.*

**13**    *A reading from the second letter of St Paul to Timothy*     *(2:8-13)*

*If we die with him, then we shall live with him.*

Remember the Good News that I carry, 'Jesus Christ risen from the dead, sprung from the race of David'; it is on account of this that I have my own hardships to bear, even to being chained like a criminal - but they cannot chain up God's news. So I bear it all for the sake of those who are chosen so that in the end they may have the salvation that is in Christ Jesus and the eternal glory that comes with it. Here is a saying that you can rely on:

> If we have died with him, then we shall live with him.
> If we hold firm, then we shall reign with him.
> If we disown him, then he will disown us.
> We may be unfaithful, but he is always faithful,
> for he cannot disown his own self.

*This is the word of the Lord.*

**14**    *A reading from the first letter of St John*     *(3:1-2)*

*We shall see him as he really is.*

Think of the love that the Father has lavished on us,
by letting us be called God's children;
and that is what we are.
Because the world refused to acknowledge him,
therefore it does not acknowledge us.
My dear people, we are already the children of God
but what we are to be in the future has not yet been revealed;
all we know is, that when it is revealed
we shall be like him
because we shall see him as he really is.

*This is the word of the Lord.*

**15**    *A reading from the first letter of St John*     *(3:14-16)*

*We have passed out of death and into life because we love our brothers.*

We have passed out of death and into life,
and of this we can be sure
because we love our brothers.
    If you refuse to love, you must remain dead;
to hate your brother is to be a murderer,
and murderers, as you know, do not have eternal life in them.
This has taught us love -
that he gave up his life for us;
and we, too, ought to give up our lives for our brothers.

*This is the word of the Lord.*

# Gospels

## 1

Alleluia, alleluia!
Come, you whom my Father has blessed,
says the Lord;
take for your heritage the kingdom prepared for you
since the foundation of the world. Alleluia!                    *(Mt 25:34)*

**A reading from the holy Gospel according to Matthew**  *(5:1-12)*

*Rejoice and be glad, for your reward will be great in heaven.*

Seeing the crowds, Jesus went up the hill. There he sat down and was joined by his disciples. Then he began to speak. This is what he taught them:

'How happy are the poor in spirit;
theirs is the kingdom of heaven.
Happy the gentle:
they shall have the earth for their heritage.
Happy those who mourn:
they shall be comforted.
Happy those who hunger and thirst for what is right:
they shall be satisfied.
Happy the merciful:
they shall have mercy shown them.
Happy the pure in heart:
they shall see God.
Happy the peacemakers:
they shall be called sons of God.
Happy those who are persecuted in the cause of right:
theirs is the kingdom of heaven.

'Happy are you when people abuse you and persecute you and speak all kinds of calumny against you on my account. Rejoice and be glad, for your reward will be great in heaven.'

*This is the Gospel of the Lord.*

## 2

Alleluia, alleluia!
Blessed are you, Father,
Lord of heaven and earth;
for revealing the mysteries of the kingdom
to mere children.
Alleluia!

*(cf Mt 11:25)*

*A reading from the holy Gospel according to Matthew*     (11:25-30)

*Come to me, and I will give you rest.*

Jesus exclaimed, 'I bless you, Father, Lord of heaven and of earth, for hiding these things from the learned and the clever and revealing them to mere children. Yes, Father, for that is what it pleased you to do. Everything has been entrusted to me by my Father; and no one knows the Son except the Father, just as no one knows the Father except the Son and those to whom the Son chooses to reveal him. 'Come to me, all you who labour and are overburdened, and I will give you rest. Shoulder my yoke and learn from me, for I am gentle and humble in heart, and you will find rest for your souls. Yes, my yoke is easy and my burden light.'

*This is the Gospel of the Lord.*

## 3

Alleluia, alleluia!
Our homeland is in heaven,
and from heaven comes the Saviour we are waiting for,
the Lord Jesus Christ.
Alleluia!

*(cf. Phil. 3:20)*

*A reading from the holy Gospel according to Matthew*  (25:1-18)

*The bridegroom is here! Go out and meet him.*

Jesus spoke this parable to his disciples:

'The kingdom of heaven will be like this: Ten bridesmaids took their lamps and went to meet the bridegroom. Five of them were foolish and five were sensible: the foolish ones did take their lamps, but they brought no oil, whereas the sensible ones took flasks of oil as well as their lamps. The bridegroom was late and they all grew drowsy and fell asleep. But at midnight there was a cry. "The bridegroom is here! Go out and meet him." At this, all those bridesmaids woke up and trimmed their lamps, and the foolish ones said to the sensible ones, "Give us some of your oil: our lamps are going out". But they replied, "There may not be enough for us and for you; you had better go to those who sell it and buy some for yourselves". They had gone off to buy it when the bridegroom arrived. Those who were ready went in with him to the wedding hall and the door was closed. The other bridesmaids arrived later. "Lord, Lord," they said, "open the door for us." But he replied, "I tell you solemnly, I do not know you". So stay awake, because you do not know either the day or the hour.

> *This is the Gospel of the Lord.*

## 4

Alleluia, alleluia!
Come, you whom my Father has blessed,
says the Lord;
take for your heritage the kingdom prepared for you
since the foundation of the world.
Alleluia!                                                    *(Mt 25:34)*

### A reading from the holy Gospel according to Matthew  (25:31-46)

> *Come, you whom my Father has blessed*

Jesus said to his disciples: 'When the Son of Man comes in his glory, escorted by     all the angels, he will take his seat on his throne of glory. All the nations will be assembled before him and he will separate men one from another as the shepherd separates sheep from goats. He will place the sheep on his right hand and the goats on his left. Then the King will say to those on his right hand, "Come, you whom my Father has blessed, take for your heritage the kingdom prepared for you since the foundation of the world. For I was hungry and you gave me food; I was thirsty and you gave me drink; I was a stranger and you made me welcome; naked and you clothed me, sick and you visited me, in prison and you came to see me." Then the virtuous will say to him in reply, "Lord, when did we see you hungry and feed you; or thirsty and give you drink? When did we see you a stranger and make you welcome; naked and clothe you; sick or in prison and go to see you?" And the King will answer, "I tell you solemnly, in so far as you did this to one of the least of these brothers of mine, you did it to me." Next he will say to those on his left hand, "Go away from me, with your curse upon you, to the eternal fire prepared for the devil and his angels. For I was hungry and you never gave me food; I was thirsty and you never gave me anything to drink; I was a stranger and you never made me welcome, naked and you never clothed me, sick and in prison and you never visited me." Then it will be their turn to ask, "Lord when did we see you hungry or thirsty, a stranger or naked, sick or in prison, and did not come to your help?" Then he will answer, "I tell you solemnly, in so far as you neglected to do this to one of the least of these, you neglected to do it to me." And they will go away to eternal punishment, and the virtuous to eternal life.'

> *This is the Gospel of the Lord.*

## 5

Alleluia, alleluia!
If we have died with Christ; then we shall live with him;
if we hold firm, then we shall reign with him.
Alleluia!

*(2 Tim 2:11-12)*

**A reading from the holy Gospel according to Mark**          *(15:33-39; 16:1-6)*

*Jesus gave a loud cry and breathed his last.*

When the sixth hour came there was darkness over the whole land until the ninth hour. And at the ninth hour Jesus cried out in a loud voice, 'Eloi, Eloi, lama sabachthani?' which means, 'My God, my God, why have you deserted me?' When some of those who stood by heard this, they said, 'Listen, he is calling on Elijah.' Someone ran and soaked a sponge in vinegar and, putting it on a reed, gave it him to drink saying, 'Wait and see if Elijah will come to take him down.' But Jesus gave a loud cry and breathed his last. And the veil of the Temple was torn in two from top to bottom. The centurion, who was standing in front of him, had seen how he had died and he said, 'In truth this man was a son of God.'

When the sabbath was over, Mary of Magdala, Mary the mother of James, and Salome, bought spices with which to go and anoint him. And very early in the morning on the first day of the week they went to the tomb, just as the sun was rising.

They had been saying to one another, 'Who will roll away the stone for us from the entrance to the tomb?' But when they looked they could see that the stone - which was very big - had already been rolled back. On entering the tomb they saw a young man in a white robe seated on the right-hand side, and they were struck with amazement. But he said to them, 'There is no need for alarm. You are looking for Jesus of Nazareth, who was crucified: he has risen, he is not here. See, here is the place where they laid him.'

*This is the Gospel of the Lord.*

---

SHORTER FORM

**A reading from the holy Gospel according to Mark**          *(15:33-39)*

*Jesus gave a loud cry and breathed his last.*

When the sixth hour came there was darkness over the whole land until the ninth hour. And at the ninth hour Jesus cried out in a loud voice, 'Eloi, Eloi, lama sabachthani?' which means, 'My God, my God, why have you deserted me?' When some of those who stood by heard this, they said, 'Listen, he is calling on Elijah.' Someone ran and soaked a sponge in vinegar and putting it on a reed, gave it him to drink saying, 'Wait and see if Elijah will come to take him down.' But Jesus gave a loud cry and breathed his last. And the veil of the Temple was torn in two from top to bottom. The centurion, who was standing in front of him, had seen how he had died and he said, 'In truth this man was a son of God.'

*This is the Gospel of the Lord.*

## 6

Alleluia, alleluia!
I am the resurrection and the life,
says the Lord:
whoever believes in me will never die.
Alleluia!

*(Jn 11:25-26)*

*A reading from the holy Gospel according to Luke*     *(7:11-17)*

*Young man, I tell you to get up.*

Jesus went to a town called Nain, accompanied by his disciples and a great number of people. When he was near the gate of the town it happened that a dead man was being carried out for burial, the only son of his mother, and she was a widow. And a considerable number of the townspeople were with her. When the Lord saw her he felt sorry for her. 'Do not cry,' he said. Then he went up and put his hand on the bier and the bearers stood still, and he said, 'Young man, I tell you to get up'. And the dead man sat up and began to talk, and Jesus gave him to his mother. Everyone was filled with awe and praised God saying, 'A great prophet has appeared among us; God has visited his people'. And this opinion of him spread throughout Judaea and all over the countryside.

*This is the Gospel of the Lord.*

## 7

Alleluia, alleluia!
Our homeland is in heaven,
and from heaven comes the Saviour we are waiting for,
the Lord Jesus Christ.
Alleluia!

*(cf. Phil 3:20)*

*A reading from the holy Gospel according to Luke*     *(12:35-40)*

*Stand ready.*

Jesus said to his disciples: 'See that you are dressed for action and have your lamps lit. Be like men waiting for their master to return from the wedding feast, ready to open the door as soon as he comes and knocks. Happy those servants whom the master finds awake when he comes. I tell you solemnly, he will put on an apron, sit them down at table and wait on them. It may be in the second watch he comes, or in the third, but happy those servants if he finds them ready. You may be quite sure of this, that if the householder had known at what hour the burglar would come, he would not have let anyone break through the wall of his house. You too must stand ready, because the Son of Man is coming at an hour you do not expect.'

*This is the Gospel of the Lord.*

## 8

Alleluia, alleluia!
Happy are those who die in the Lord.
Now they can rest for ever after their work,
since their good deeds go with them.
Alleluia!

*(Apoc 14:13)*

**A reading from the holy Gospel according to Luke**          *(23:33.39-43)*

*Today you will be with me in paradise.*

When the soldiers reached the place called The Skull, they crucified Jesus there and the two criminals also, one on the right, the other on the left.

One of the criminals hanging there abused him. 'Are you not the Christ?' he said. Save yourself and us as well.' But the other spoke up and rebuked him. 'Have you no fear of God at all?' he said. 'You got the same sentence as he did, but in our case we deserved it: we are paying for what we did. But this man has done nothing wrong. Jesus,' he said, 'Remember me when you come into your kingdom.' 'Indeed, I promise you,' he replied, 'Today you will be with me in paradise.'

*This is the Gospel of the Lord.*

## 9

Alleluia, alleluia!
Jesus Christ is the First-bom from the dead;
to him be glory and power for ever and ever. Amen.
Alleluia!

*(Apoc 1:5-6)*

**A reading from the holy Gospel according to Luke**          *(23:44-46.50.52-53; 24:1-6)*

*Father, into your hands I commend my spirit.*

It was about the sixth hour and, with the sun eclipsed, a darkness came over the whole land until the ninth hour. The veil of the temple was torn right down the middle; and when Jesus had cried out in a loud voice, he said, 'Father, into your hands I commit my spirit'. With these words he breathed his last.

Then a member of the council arrived, an upright and virtuous man named Joseph. This man went to Pilate and asked for the body of Jesus. He then took it down, wrapped it in a shroud and put him in a tomb which was hewn in stone in which no one had yet been laid. On the first day of the week, at the first sign of dawn, the women went to the tomb with the spices they had prepared. They found that the stone had been rolled away from the tomb, but on entering discovered that the body of the Lord Jesus was not there. As they stood there not knowing what to think, two men in brilliant clothes suddenly appeared at their side. Terrified, the women lowered their eyes. But the two men said to them.'Why look among the dead for someone who is alive? He is not here; he has risen.'

*This is the Gospel of the Lord.*

SHORTER FORM

*A reading from the holy Gospel according to Luke*          (23:44-46.50.52-53)

*Father, into your hands I comend my spirit.*

It was about the sixth hour and with the sun eclipsed, a darkness came over the whole land until the ninth hour. The veil of the Temple was torn right down the middle, and when Jesus had cried out in a loud voice, he said, 'Father, into your hands I commit my spirit'. With these words he breathed his last.

Then a member of the council arrived, an upright and virtuous man named Joseph. This man went to Pilate and asked for the body of Jesus. He then took it down, wrapped it in a shroud and put him in a tomb which was hewn in stone in which no one had yet been laid.

*This is the Gospel of the Lord.*

## 10

Alleluia, alleluia!
God loved the world so much
that he gave his only Son;
everyone who believes in him has eternal life.
Alleluia!                                                                 *(Jn 3:16)*

*A reading from the holy Gospel according to Luke*          (24:13-35)

*Was it not ordained that the Christ should suffer and enter into his glory?*

On the first day of the week, two of the disciples were on their way to a village called Emmaus, seven miles from Jerusalem, and they were talking together about all that had happened. Now as they talked this over, Jesus himself came up and walked by their side; but something prevented them from recognising him. He said to them, 'What matters are you discussing as you walk along?' They stopped short, their faces downcast.

Then one of them, called Cleopas, answered him, 'You must be the only person stay-ing in Jerusalem who does not know the things that have been happening there these last few days.' 'What things?' he asked. 'All about Jesus of Nazareth,' they answered, 'who proved he was a great prophet by the things he said and did in the sight of God and of the whole people; and how our chief priests and our leaders handed him over to be sentenced to death, and had him crucified. Our own hope had been that he would be the one to set Israel free. And this is not all: two whole days have gone by since it all happened: and some women from our group have astounded us; they went to the tomb in the early morning, and when they did not find the body, they came back to tell us they had seen a vision of angels who declared he was alive. Some of our friends went to the tomb and found everything exactly as the women had reported, but of him they saw nothing. Then he said to them, 'You foolish men! So slow to believe the full message of the prophets! Was it not ordained that the Christ should suffer and so enter into his glory?' Then, starting with Moses and going through all the prophets, he explained to them the passages throughout the scriptures that were about himself.

When they drew near to the village to which they were going, he made as if to go on; but they pressed him to stay with them. 'It is nearly evening,' they said, 'and the day is almost over.' So he went in to stay with them. Now while he was with them at table, he took the bread and said the blessing; then he broke it and handed it to them. And their eyes were opened and they recognised him; but he had vanished from their sight. Then they said to each other, 'Did not our hearts burn within us as he talked to us on the road and explained the scriptures to us?' They set out that instant and returned to Jerusalem. There they found the Eleven assembled together with their companions, who said to them, 'Yes, it is true. The Lord has risen and has appeared to Simon.' Then they told their story of what had happened on the road and how they had recognised him at the breaking of bread.

*This is the Gospel of the Lord.*

SHORTER FORM

## *A reading from the holy Gospel according to Luke*　　　(21:13-16. 28-35)

*Was it not ordained that the Christ should suffer and enter into his glory?*

On the first day of the week, two of the disciples were on their way to a village called Emmaus, seven miles from Jerusalem, and they were talking together about all that had happened. Now as they talked this over, Jesus himself came up and walked by their side; but something prevented them from recognising him.

When they drew near to the village to which they were going, he made as if to go on; but they pressed him to stay with them. 'It is nearly evening,' they said, 'and the day is almost over.' So he went in to stay with them. Now while he was with them at table, he took the bread and said the blessing; then he broke it and handed it to them. And their eyes were opened and they recognised him; but he had vanished from their sight. Then they said to each other, 'Did not our hearts burn within us as he talked to us on the road and explained the scriptures to us?'

They set out that instant and returned to Jerusalem. There they found the Eleven assembled together with their companions, who said to them, 'Yes it is true. The Lord has risen and has appeared to Simon.' Then they told their story of what had happened on the road and how they had recognised him at the breaking of bread.

*This is the Gospel of the Lord.*

## 11

Alleluia, alleluia!
Come, you whom my Father has blessed,
says the Lord;
take for your heritage the kingdom prepared for you
since the foundation of the world.
Alleluia!

*(Mt 25:34)*

*A reading from the holy Gospel according to John (5:24-29)*

*Whoever listens to my words and believes has passed from death to life.*

Jesus said to the Jews:
'I tell you most solemnly,
whoever listens to my words,
and believes in the one who sent me,
has eternal life;
without being brought to judgement
he has passed from death to life.
I tell you most solemnly,
the hour will come - in fact it is here already -
when the dead will hear the voice of the Son of God,
and all who hear it will live.
For the Father, who is the source of life,
has made the Son the source of life;
and, because he is the Son of Man,
has appointed him supreme judge.
Do not be suprised at this,
for the hour is coming
when the dead will leave their graves
at the sound of his voice;
those who did good will rise again to life;
and those who did evil, to condemnation.
I can do nothing by myself;
I can only judge as I am told to judge,
and my judging is just,
because my aim is to do not my own will,
but the will of him who sent me.'

*This is the Gospel of the Lord.*

## 12

Alleluia, alleluia!
It is my Father's will, says the Lord,
that I should lose nothing of all that he has given to me,
and that I should raise it up on the last day.
Alleluia!                                                        *(Jn 6:39)*

### A reading from the holy Gospel according to John          (6:37-20)

*Whoever believes in the Son has eternal life, and I shall raise him up on the last day.*

Jesus said to the crowd:
'All that the Father gives me will come to me,
and whoever comes to me
I shall not turn him away;
because I have come from heaven,
not to do my own will,
but to do the will of the one who sent me.
Now the will of him who sent me
is that I should lose nothing
of all that he has given to me,
and that I should raise it up on the last day.
Yes, it is my Father's will
that whoever sees the Son and believes in him
shall have eternal life,
and that I shall raise him up on the last day.'

*This is the Gospel of the Lord.*

## 13

Alleluia, alleluia!
I am the living bread
which has come down from heaven,
says the Lord.
Anyone who eats this bread
will live for ever.
Alleluia!                                                        *(Jn 6:51-52)*

### A reading from the holy Gospel according to John          (6:51-68)

*Anyone who eats this bread has eternal life, and I shall raise him up on the last day.*

Jesus said to the crowd:
'I am the living bread which has come down from heaven.
Anyone who eats this bread will live for ever;

and the bread that I shall give is my flesh,
for the life of the world.'

Then the Jews started arguing with one another: 'How can this man give us his flesh to eat?' they said. Jesus replied:

'I tell you most solemnly,
if you do not eat the flesh of the Son of Man
and drink his blood,
you will not have life in you.
Anyone who does eat my flesh and drink my blood
has eternal life, and I shall raise him up on the last day.
For my flesh is real food
and my blood is real drink.
He who eats my flesh and drinks my blood
lives in me
and I live in him.
As I, who am sent by the living Father,
myself draw life from the Father,
so whoever eats me will draw life from me.
This is the bread come down from heaven;
not like the bread our ancestors ate:
they are dead,
but anyone who eats this bread will live for ever.'

*This is the Gospel of the Lord.*

## 14

Alleluia, alleluia!
I am the resurrection and the life, says the Lord,
whoever believes in me will never die.
Alleluia!                                                    *(Jn 11:25 2ff)*

### A reading from the holy Gospel according to John          (11:17-27)

*I am the resurrection and the life.*

On arriving at Bethany, Jesus found that Lazarus had been in the tomb for four days already. Bethany is only about two miles from Jerusalem, and many Jews had come to Martha and Mary to sympathise with them over their brother. When Martha heard that Jesus had come she went to meet him. Mary remained sitting in the house. Martha said to Jesus, 'If you had been here, my brother would not have died, but I know that, even now, whatever you ask of God, he will grant you'. 'Your brother,' said Jesus to her, 'will rise again.' Martha said, 'I know he will rise again at the resurrection on the last day'. Jesus said:

'I am the resurrection and the life.

If anyone believes in me,
even though he dies he will live,
and whoever lives and believes in me
will never die.
Do you believe this?'

'Yes, Lord,' she said, 'I believe that you are the Christ, the Son of God, the one who was to come into this world.'

*This is the Gospel of the Lord.*

---

SHORTER FORM

## A reading from the holy Gospel according to John (11:21-27)

*I am the resurrection and the life.*

Martha said to Jesus, 'If you had been here, my brother would not have died, but I know that, now, whatever you ask of God, he will grant you'. 'Your brother,' said Jesus to her, 'will rise again.' Martha said, 'I know he will rise again at the resurrection on the last day'. Jesus said:

'I am the resurrection and the life.
If anyone believes in me,
even though he dies he will live,
and whoever lives and believes in me
will never die.
Do you believe this?'

'Yes, Lord,' she said, 'I believe that you are the Christ, the Son of God, the one who was to come into this world.'

*This is the Gospel of the Lord.*

---

## 15

Alleluia, alleluia!
God loved the world so much
that he gave his only Son;
everyone who believes in him has eternal life.
Alleluia!

*Jn 3:16*

## A reading from the holy Gospel according to John (11:32-45)

*Lazarus, come out.*

Mary the sister of Lazarus went to Jesus, and as soon as she saw him she threw herself at his feet, saying, 'Lord, if you had been here, my brother would not have died.' At the sight of her tears, and those of the Jews who followed her, Jesus said in great distress, with a sigh that came straight from the heart, 'Where have you put him?' They said,

'Lord, come and see'. Jesus wept; and the Jews said, 'See how much he loved him!' But there were some who remarked, 'He opened the eyes of the blind man, could he not have prevented this man's death?' Still sighing, Jesus reached the tomb: it was a cave with a stone to close the opening. Jesus said, 'Take the stone away.' Martha said to him, 'Lord, by now he will smell; this is the fourth day.' Jesus replied, 'Have I not told you that if you believe you will see the glory of God?' So they took away the stone. Then Jesus lifted up his eyes and said:

> 'Father, I thank you for hearing my prayer.
> I knew indeed that you always hear me,
> but I speak
> for the sake of all these who stand round me,
> so that they may believe it was you who sent me.'

When he had said this, he cried in a loud voice, 'Lazarus, here! Come out!' The dead man came out, his feet and hands bound with bands of stuff and a cloth round his face. Jesus said to them, 'Unbind him, let him go free.'

Many of the Jews who had come to visit Mary and had seen what he did believed in him.

*This is the Gospel of the Lord.*

### 16

Alleluia, alleluia!
Happy are those who die in the Lord!
Now they can rest for ever after their work,
since their good deeds go with them.
Alleluia!                                                    *(Apoc 14:13)*

**A reading from the holy Gospel according to John  (12:23-28)**

*If a wheat grain dies, it yields a rich harvest.*
Jesus said to his disciples:
> 'Now the hour has come
> for the Son of Man to be glorified.
> I tell you, most solemnly,
> unless a wheat grain falls on the ground and dies,
> it remains only a single grain;
> but if it dies,
> it yields a rich harvest.
> Anyone who loves his life loses it;
> anyone who hates his life in this world
> will keep it for the eternal life.
> If a man serves me, he must follow me,
> wherever I am my servant will be there too.

If anyone serves me, my Father will honour him.
Now my soul is troubled.
What shall I say:
Father, save me from this hour?
But it is for this very reason that I have come to this hour.
Father, glorify your name!'

A voice came from heaven, 'I have glorified it, and I will glorify it again.'

*This is the Gospel of the Lord.*

SHORTER FORM

**A reading from the holy Gospel according to John (12:23-26)**

*If a wheat grain dies, it yields a rich harvest.*
Jesus said to his disciples:
'Now the hour has come
for the Son of Man to be glorified.
I tell you, most solemnly,
unless a wheat grain falls on the ground and dies,
it remains only a single grain;
but if it dies, it yields a rich harvest.
Anyone who loves his life loses it;
anyone who hates his life in this world
will keep it for the eternal life.
If a man serves me, he must follow me,
wherever I am, my servant will be there too
If anyone serves me, my Father will honour him.'

*This is the Gospel of the Lord.*

## 17

Alleluia, alleluia!
It is my Father's will, says the Lord,
that whoever believes in the Son
shall have eternal life:
and that I shall raise him up on the last day.
Alleluia!

*(Jn 6:40)*

**A reading from the holy Gospel according to John (14:1-6)**

*There are many rooms in my Father's house.*
Jesus said to his disciples:
'Do not let your hearts be troubled.
Trust in God still, and trust in me.

57

There are many rooms in my Father's house;
if there were not, I should have told you.
I am going now to prepare a place for you,
and after I have gone and prepared you a place,
I shall return to take you with me;
so that where I am
you may be too.
You know the way to the place where I am going.

Thomas said, 'Lord, we do not know where you are going, so how can we know the way?' Jesus said:

'I am the Way, the Truth and the Life.
No one can come to the Father except through me.'

*This is the Gospel of the Lord.*

## 18

Alleluia, alleluia!
It is my Father's will, says the Lord,
that I should lose nothing
of all that he has given to me,
and that I should raise it up on the last day.
Alleluia!                                            *(Jn 6:39)*

**A reading from the holy Gospel according to John (17:24-26)**

*I want them to be with me where I am.*
Jesus raised his eyes to heaven and said:
'Father,
I want those you have given me
to be with me where I am,
so that they may always see the glory
you have given me
because you loved me
before the foundation of the world.
Father, Righteous One,
the world has not known you,
but I have known you,
and these have known
that you have sent me.
I have made your name known to them
and will continue to make it known
so that the love with which you loved me may be in them,
and so that I may be in them.'

*This is the Gospel of the Lord.*

## 19

Alleluia, alleluia!
I am the resurrection and the life,
says the Lord,
whoever believes in me will never die.
Alleluia!

*(Jn 11:25 26)*

### A reading from the holy Gospel according to John (19:17-18.25-30)

*Bowing his head he gave up his spirit.*

Carrying his own cross, Jesus went out of the city to the place of the skull or, as it was called in Hebrew, Golgotha, where they crucified him with two others, one on either side with Jesus in the middle. Near the cross of Jesus stood his mother and his mother's sister, Mary the wife of Clopas, and Mary of Magdala. Seeing his mother and the disciple he loved standing near her, Jesus said to his mother, 'Woman, this is your son'. Then to the disciple he said, 'This is your mother'.

After this, Jesus knew that everything had now been completed, and to fulfil the scripture perfectly he said:

'I am thirsty'.

A jar full of vinegar stood there, so putting a sponge soaked in the vinegar on a hyssop stick they held it up to his mouth. After Jesus had taken the vinegar he said, 'It is accomplished'; and bowing his head he gave up his spirit.

It was Preparation Day, and to prevent the bodies remaining on the cross during sabbath - since that sabbath was a day of special solemnity - the Jews asked Pilate to have the legs broken and the bodies taken away. Consequently the soldiers came and broke the legs of the first man who had been crucified with him and then of the other. When they came to Jesus, they found he was already dead, and so instead of breaking his legs one of the soldiers pierced his side with a lance; and immediately there came out blood and water. This is the evidence of one who saw it - trustworthy evidence, and he knows he speaks the truth and he gives it so that you may believe as well. Because all this happened to fulfil the words of scripture:

Not one bone of his will be broken;

and again, in another place scripture says:

They will look on the one whom they have pierced.

After this, Joseph of Arimathaea, who was a disciple of Jesus - though a secret one because he was afraid of the Jews - asked Pilate to let him remove the body of Jesus. Pilate gave permission, so they came and took it away. Nicodemus came as well - the same one who had first come to Jesus at night-time - and he brought a mixture of myrrh and aloes weighing about a hundred pounds.

*This is the Gospel of the Lord.*

# Prayers for the funeral rite

# Prayers for the Dead used in the Funeral Rite

*These prayers are used at various times during the funeral, for instance as opening prayers at Mass or Funeral Service, and at the Vigil. A wide selection of prayers is given, as listed here.*

## General prayers

1 God of faithfulness,
in your wisdom you have called
your servant N. out of this world;
release him/her from the bonds of sin,
and welcome him/her into your presence,
so that he/she may enjoy eternal light
and peace
and be raised up in glory with all your
saints.

We ask this through Christ our Lord.
**Amen.**

2 Lord, in our grief we turn to you.
Are you not the God of love
always ready to hear our cries?

Listen to our prayers for your servant N,
whom you have called out of this world:
lead him/her to your kingdom of light
and peace
and count him/her among the saints in
glory.

We ask this through Christ our Lord.
**Amen.**

3 Holy Lord, almighty and eternal God,
hear our prayers for your servant N.
whom you have summoned out of this
world.

Forgive his/her sins and failings
and grant him/her a place of refreshment,
light, and peace.
Let him/her pass unharmed through the
gates of death
to dwell with the blessed in light,
as you promised to Abraham and his
children for ever.
Accept N. into your safe-keeping
and on the great day of judgment
raise him/her up with all the saints
to inherit your eternal kingdom.

We ask this through Christ our Lord.

**Amen.**

4  Into your hands, O Lord,
   we humbly entrust our brother/sister N.
   In this life you embraced him/her with
      your tender love;
   deliver him/her now from every evil
   and bid him/her enter eternal rest.

   The old order has passed away:
   welcome him/her then into paradise,
   where there will be no sorrow, no
      weeping nor pain,
   but the fullness of peace and joy
   with your Son and the Holy Spirit for ever
      and ever.
   **Amen.**

5  Almighty God and Father,
   it is our certain faith
   that your Son, who died on the cross, was
      raised from the dead,
   the firstfruits of all who have fallen asleep.
   Grant that through this mystery
   your servant N. who has gone to his/her
   rest in Christ,
   may share in the joy of his resurrection.

   We ask this through Christ our Lord.
   **Amen.**

6  O God,
   glory of believers and life of the just,
   by the death and resurrection of your Son,
      we are redeemed:
   have mercy on your servant N.,
   and make him/her worthy to share the
      joys of paradise,
   for he/she believed in the resurrection
   of the dead.

   We ask this through Christ our Lord.
   **Amen.**

7  Almighty God and Father,
   by the mystery of the cross, you have
      made us strong;

by the sacrament of the resurrection
you have sealed us as your own.
Look kindly upon your servant N.,
now freed from the bonds of mortality,
and count him/her among your saints
   in heaven.

We ask this through Christ our Lord.
**Amen.**

8  God of loving kindness,
   listen favourably to our prayers:
   strengthen our belief that your Son has
      risen from the dead
   and our hope that your servant N. will
      also rise again.

   We ask this through Christ our Lord.
   **Amen.**

9  To you, O God, the dead do not die,
   and in death our life is changed,
      not ended.
   Hear our prayers
   and command the soul of your servant N.
   to dwell with Abraham, your friend,
   and be raised at last on the great day of
      judgement.
   In your mercy cleanse him/her of any sin
   which he/she may have committed
      through human frailty.

   We ask this through Christ our Lord.
   **Amen.**

10 Lord God, in whom all find refuge,
   we appeal to your boundless mercy:
   grant to the soul of your servant N.
   a kindly welcome,
   cleansing of sin,
   release from the chains of death,
   and entry into everlasting life.

   We ask this through Christ our Lord.
   **Amen.**

11  God of all consolation,
 open our hearts to your word,
 so that, listening to it, we may comfort
  one another,
 finding light in time of darkness
 and faith in time of doubt.

 We ask this through Christ our Lord.
 **Amen.**

12  O God,
 to whom mercy and forgiveness belong,
 hear our prayers on behalf of your
  servant N.,
 whom you have called out of this world;
 and because he/she put his/her hope and
  trust in you,
 command that he/she be carried safely
  home to heaven
 and come to enjoy your eternal reward.

 We ask this through Christ our Lord.
 **Amen.**

13  O God,
 in whom sinners find mercy and the
  saints find joy,
 we pray to you for our brother/sister N.,
 whose body we honour with Christian
  burial,
 that he/she may be delivered from the
 bonds of death.
 Admit him/her to the joyful company of
  your saints
 and raise him/her on the last day
 to rejoice in your presence for ever.

 We ask this through Christ our Lord.

 **Amen.**

## For a priest

17  God of mercy and love,
 grant to N., your servant and priest,
 a glorious place at your heavenly table,
 for you made him here on earth
 a faithful minister of your word and
  sacrament.

 We ask this through Christ our Lord.
 **Amen.**

18  O God,
 listen favourably to our prayers
 offered on behalf of your servant and priest,
 and grant that N.,
 who committed himself zealously to the
  service of your name,
 may rejoice for ever in the company
  of your saints.

 We ask this through Christ our Lord.
 **Amen.**

19  Lord God,
 you chose our brother N. to serve your
  people as a priest
 and to share the joys and burdens of their
  lives.

 Look with mercy on him
 and give him the reward of his labours,
 the fulness of life promised to those who
  preach your holy Gospel.

 We ask this through Christ our Lord.
 **Amen.**

## For a deacon

**20** God of mercy,
as once you chose seven men of honest
repute
to serve your Church,
so also you chose N. as your servant and
deacon.
Grant that he may rejoice in your eternal
fellowship
with all the heralds of your Gospel,
for he was untiring in his ministry here on
earth.

We ask this through Christ our Lord.
**Amen.**

**21** Lord God,
you sent your Son into the world
to preach the Good News of salvation
and to pour out his Spirit of grace upon
your Church.

Look with kindness on your servant N.
As a deacon in the Church
he was strengthened by the gift of the Spirit
to preach the Good News,
to minister in your assembly,
and to do the works of charity.

Give him the reward promised
to those who show their love of you
by service to their neighbour.

We ask this through Christ our Lord.
**Amen.**

## For a religious

**22** All-powerful God,
we pray for our brother/sister N.,
who responded to the call of Christ
and pursued wholeheartedly the ways of
perfect love.
Grant that he/she may rejoice
on that day when your glory will be
revealed
and in company with all his/her brothers
and sisters
share for ever the happiness of your
kingdom.

We ask this through Christ our Lord.
**Amen.**

**23** God of blessings,
source of all holiness,
the voice of your Spirit has drawn countless
men and women
to follow Jesus Christ
and to bind themselves to you with ready
will and loving heart.

Look with mercy on N.
who sought to fulfill his/her vows to you,
and grant him/her the reward promised to
all good and faithful servants.

May he/she rejoice in the company of the
saints
and with them praise you for ever.

We ask this through Christ our Lord.
**Amen.**

## For one who worked in the service of the Gospel

**24** Faithful God,
we humbly ask your mercy for your servant N.,
who worked so generously to spread the Good News:
grant him/her the reward of his/her labours
and bring him/her safely to your promised land.

We ask this through Christ our Lord.
**Amen.**

## For a baptized child

25 Lord, in our grief we call upon your mercy:
   open your ears to our prayers,
   and one day unite us again with N.
   who, we firmly trust,
   already enjoys eternal life in your kingdom.

   We ask this through Christ our Lord.
   **Amen.**

26 To you, O Lord,
   we humbly entrust this child,
   so precious in your sight.
   Take him/her into your arms
   and welcome him/her into paradise,
   where there will be no sorrow, no
      weeping nor pain,
   but the fullness of peace and joy
   with your Son and the Holy Spirit for
      ever and ever.
   **Amen.**

## For a young person

27 Lord,
   your wisdom governs the length of our
      days.
   We mourn the loss of N.
   whose life has passed so quickly,
   and we entrust him/her to your mercy.
   Welcome him/her into your heavenly
      dwelling
   and grant him/her the happiness of
      everlasting youth.

   We ask this through Christ our Lord.
   **Amen.**

28 Lord God,
   source and destiny of our lives,
   in your loving providence
   you gave us N.
   to grow in wisdom, age, and grace.
   Now you have called him/her to yourself.
   As we grieve the loss of one so young,
   we seek to understand your purpose.
   Draw him/her to yourself
   and give him/her full stature in Christ.
   May he/she stand with all the angels and
      saints,
   who know your love and praise your
      saving will.

   We ask this through Christ our Lord.
   **Amen.**

## 29    Parents

Lord, God, who commanded us to
honour father and mother,
look kindly upon your servants N. and N.,
have mercy upon them and let us see them
     again in eternal light.

We ask this through Christ our Lord.
**Amen.**

## 30    A parent

God of our ancestors in faith,
by the covenant made on Mount Sinai
you taught your people to strengthen the
     bonds of family
through faith, honour, and love.
Look kindly upon N.,
a father/mother who sought to bind
     his/her children to you.
Bring him/her one day to our heavenly
     home
where the saints dwell in blessedness and
     peace.

We ask this through Christ our Lord.
**Amen.**

## For a married couple

31   Lord God, whose covenant is everlasting,
have mercy upon the sins of your
     servants N.and N.;
as their love for each other united them
     on earth,
so let your love join them together in
     heaven.

We ask this through Christ our Lord.
**Amen.**

32   Eternal Father
in the beginning you established the love
     of man and woman
as a sign of creation.
Your own Son loves the Church as a
     spouse.
Grant mercy and peace to N. and N. who,
by their love for each other,
were signs of the creative love
which binds the Church to Christ.

We ask this through Christ our Lord.
**Amen.**

33   Lord God,
giver of all that is true and lovely and
     gracious,
you created in marriage a sign of your
     covenant.
Look with mercy upon N. and N.
You blessed them in their companionship,
and in their joys and sorrows you bound
     them together.
Lead them into eternal peace,
and bring them to the table
where the saints feast together in your
     heavenly home.

We ask this through Christ our Lord.
**Amen.**

## 34    A wife

Eternal God,
 you made the love of man and woman
a sign of the bond between Christ and
   the Church.

Grant mercy and peace to N.,
who was united in love with her husband.
May the care and devotion of her life
   on earth
find a lasting reward in heaven.
Look kindly on her husband and
   family/children
as now they turn to your compassion
   and love.
Strengthen their faith and lighten their loss.

We ask this through Christ our Lord.
**Amen.**

## 35    A husband

Eternal God,
 you made the love of man and woman
a sign of the bond between Christ and the
   Church.

Grant mercy and peace to N.,
who was united in love with his wife.
May the care and devotion of his life
   on earth
find a lasting reward in heaven.
Look kindly on his wife and
   family/children
as now they turn to your compassion and
   love.
 Strengthen their faith and lighten their loss.

We ask this through Christ our Lord.
**Amen.**

## 36    A non-Christian married to a Catholic

Almighty and faithful Creator,
all things are of your making,
all people are shaped in your image.
We now entrust the soul of N. to your goodness.
In your infinite wisdom and power,
work in him/her your merciful purpose,
known to you alone from the beginning of time.
Console the hearts of those who love him/her
in the hope that all who trust in you
will find peace and rest in your kingdom.

We ask this through Christ our Lord.
**Amen.**

### An elderly person

37 God of endless ages,
 from one generation to the next
 you have been our refuge and strength.
 Before the mountains were born
 or the earth came to be,
 you are God.
 Have mercy now on your servant N.
 whose long life was spent in your service.
 Give him/her a place in your kingdom,
 where hope is firm for all who love
 and rest is sure for all who serve.

 We ask this through Christ our Lord.
 **Amen.**

38 God of mercy,
 look kindly on your servant N.
 who has set down the burden of his/her
 years.
 As he/she served you faithfully
 throughout his/her life,
 may you give him/her the fullness of your
 peace and joy.
 We give thanks for the long life of N.,
 now caught up in your eternal love.

 We ask this through Christ our Lord.
 **Amen.**

### One who died after a long illness

39 God of deliverance,
 you called our brother/sister N.
 to serve you in weakness and pain,
 and gave him/her the grace of sharing the
 cross of your Son.
 Reward his/her patience and forbearance,
 and grant him/her the fullness of Christ's
 victory.

 We ask this through Christ our Lord.
 **Amen.**

40 Most faithful God,
 lively is the courage of those who
 hope in you.
 Your servant N. suffered greatly
 but placed his/her trust in your mercy.
 Confident that the petition of those who
 mourn
 pierces the clouds and finds an answer,
 we beg you, give rest to N.
 Do not remember his/her sins
 but look upon his/her sufferings
 and grant him/her refreshment, light,
 and peace.

 We ask this through Christ our Lord.
 **Amen.**

41 O God,
 you are water for our thirst
 and manna in our desert.
 We praise you for the life of N.
 and bless your mercy
 that has brought his/her suffering to an end.
 Now we beg that same endless mercy
 to raise him/her to new life.
 Nourished by the food and drink of
 heaven,
 may he/she rest for ever in the joy of
 Christ our Lord.
 **Amen.**

**42    One who died suddenly**

Lord, as we mourn the sudden death of
  our brother/sister,
show us the immense power of your
  goodness
and strengthen our belief
that N. has entered into your presence.

We ask this through Christ our Lord.
**Amen.**

**43    One who died accidentally or violently**

Lord our God,
you are always faithful and quick
to show mercy.
Our brother/sister N.
was suddenly [and violently] taken from us.
Come swiftly to his/her aid,
have mercy on him/her,
and comfort his/her family and friends
by the power and protection of the cross.

We ask this through Christ our Lord.
**Amen.**

**One who died by suicide**

44  God, lover of souls,
  you hold dear what you have made
  and spare all things, for they are yours.
  Look gently on your servant N.,
  and by the blood of the cross
  forgive his/her sins and failings.
  Remember the faith of those who mourn
  and satisfy their longing for that day
  when all will be made new again
  in Christ, our risen Lord,
  who lives and reigns with you for ever
  and ever.
  **Amen.**

45  Almighty God and Father of all,
  you strengthen us by the mystery of the
    cross
  and with the sacrament of your Son's
    resurrection.
  Have mercy on our brother/sister N.
  Forgive all his/her sins and grant
    him/her peace.
  May we who mourn this sudden death
    be comforted
  and consoled by your power and protection.

  We ask this through Christ our Lord.
  **Amen.**

**Several people**

46  O Lord,
  you gave new life to N. and N.
  in the waters of baptism;
  show mercy to them now,
  and bring them to the happiness of life in
    your kingdom.

  We ask this through Christ our Lord.
  **Amen.**

47  All-powerful God,
  whose mercy is never withheld
  from those who call upon you in hope,
  look kindly on your servants N. and N.,
  who departed this life confessing your
    name,
  and number them among your saints for
    evermore.

  We ask this through Christ our Lord.
  **Amen.**

# Prayers for the Mourners

*These prayers are used at various times during the funeral, for instance as opening prayers at Mass or Funeral Service, and at the Vigil. A wide selection of prayers is given, as listed here.*

## General

1 Father of mercies and God of all consolation,
you pursue us with untiring love
and dispel the shadow of death
with the bright dawn of life.

[Comfort your family in their loss and
sorrow.
Be our refuge and our strength, O Lord,
and lift us from the depths of grief
into the peace and light of your presence.]

Your Son, our Lord Jesus Christ,
by dying has destroyed our death,
and by rising, restored our life.
Enable us therefore to press on toward him,
so that, after our earthly course is run,
he may reunite us with those we love,
when every tear will be wiped away.

We ask this through Christ our Lord.
**Amen.**

2 Lord Jesus, our Redeemer,
you willingly gave yourself up to death,
so that all might be saved and pass from
death to life.
We humbly ask you to comfort your
servants in their grief
and to receive N. into the arms of your mercy.
You alone are the Holy One, you are
mercy itself;
by dying you unlocked the gates of life
for those who believe in you.
Forgive N. his/her sins,
and grant him/her a place of happiness,
light, and peace
in the kingdom of your glory for ever.
**Amen.**

3 God, all-compassionate,
ruler of the living and the dead,
you know beforehand
those whose faithful lives reveal them as your own.
We pray for those who belong to this present world
and for those who have passed to the world to come:
grant them pardon for all their sins.
We ask you graciously to hear our prayer
through the intercession of all the saints
and for your mercy's sake.
For you are God, for ever and ever.
**Amen.**

4 Lord our God,
   the death of our brother/sister N.
   recalls our human condition
   and the brevity of our lives on earth.
   But for those who believe in your love
   death is not the end,
   nor does it destroy the bonds
   that you forge in our lives.
   We share the faith of your Son's disciples
   and the hope of the children of God.
   Bring the light of Christ's resurrection
   to this time of testing and pain
   as we pray for N. and for those who love
     him/her,
   through Christ our Lord
   **Amen.**

5 Lord God,
   you are attentive to the voice of our
     pleading.

   Let us find in your Son
   comfort in our sadness,
   certainty in our doubt,
   and courage to live through this hour.
   Make our faith strong
   through Christ our Lord.
   **Amen.**

6 Lord,
   N. is gone now from this earthly dwelling
   and has left behind those who mourn
     his/her absence.
   Grant that as we grieve for our brother/sis-
     ter
   we may hold his/her memory dear
   and live in hope of the eternal kingdom
   where you will bring us together again.

   We ask this through Christ our Lord.
   **Amen.**

7 Most merciful God,
   whose wisdom is beyond our understanding,
   surround the family of N. with your love,
   that they may not be overwhelmed by their
     loss,
   but have confidence in your goodness,
   and strength to meet the days to come.

   We ask this through Christ our Lord.
   **Amen.**

## A baptized child

8 Lord of all gentleness,
   surround us with your care
   and comfort us in our sorrow,
   for we grieve at the loss of this [little] child.

   As you washed N. in the waters of baptism
   and welcomed him/her into the life of
     heaven,
   so call us one day to be united with him/her
   and share for ever the joy of your kingdom.

   We ask this through Christ our Lord.
   **Amen.**

9 Eternal Father,
   through the intercession of Mary,
   who bore your Son and stood by the
     cross as he died,
   grant to these parents in their grief
   the assistance of her presence,
   the comfort of her faith,
   and the reward of her prayers.

   We ask this through Christ our Lord.
     **Amen.**

10 Lord God, source and destiny of our lives,
in your loving providence you gave us N.
to grow in wisdom, age, and grace.
Now you have called him/her to yourself.
We grieve over the loss of one so young
and struggle to understand your purpose.
Draw him/her to yourself
and give him/her full stature in Christ.
May he/she stand with all the angels and
saints,
who know your love and praise your
saving will.
We ask this through Jesus Christ, our Lord.
**Amen.**

11 Merciful Lord,
whose wisdom is beyond human
understanding,
you adopted N. as your own in baptism
and have taken him/her to yourself
even as he/she stood on the threshold of life.
Listen to our prayers and extend to us your
grace,
that one day we may share eternal life with N.
for we firmly believe that he/she now
rests with you.

We ask this through Christ our Lord.
**Amen.**

12 Lord God,
from whom human sadness is never hidden,
you know the burden of grief
that we feel at the loss of this child.

As we mourn his/her passing from this life,
comfort us with the knowledge
that N. lives now in your loving embrace.
We ask this through Christ our Lord.
**Amen.**

## A child who died before baptism

13 O Lord, whose ways are beyond
understanding,
listen to the prayers of your faithful people:
that those weighed down by grief at the
loss of this [little] child
may find reassurance in your infinite
goodness.

We ask this through Christ our Lord.
**Amen.**

14 God of all consolation,
searcher of mind and heart,
the faith of these parents [N. and N.] is
known to you.

Comfort them with the knowledge
that the child for whom they grieve
is entrusted now to your loving care.

We ask this through Christ our Lord.
**Amen.**

## A stillborn child

15 Lord God,
ever caring and gentle,
we commit to your love this little one,
quickened to life for so short a time
Enfold him/her in eternal life.

We pray for his/her parents
who are saddened by the loss of their child.
Give them courage and help them in
their pain and grief.
May they all meet one day in the joy
and peace of your kingdom.

We ask this through Christ our Lord
**Amen.**

# Intercessions

*One of the following sets of intercessions may be used or adapted to the circumstances, or new intercessions may be composed.*

A

*The priest begins:*
God, the almighty Father, raised Christ his Son from the dead;
with confidence we ask him to save all his people, living and dead:

*A deacon or reader then continues:*
For N. who in baptism was given the pledge of eternal life, that he/she may now be admitted to the company of the saints.
Lord, in your mercy:
℟. **Hear our prayer.**

For our brother/sister who ate the body of Christ, the bread of life, that he/she may be raised up on the last day.
Lord, in your mercy:
℟. **Hear our prayer.**

For our deceased relatives and friends and for all who have helped us, that they may have the reward of their goodness.
Lord, in your mercy:
℟. **Hear our prayer.**

For those who have fallen asleep in the hope of rising again, that they may see God face to face.
Lord, in your mercy:
℟. **Hear our prayer.**

For the family and friends of our brother/sister N., that they may be consoled in their grief by the Lord, who wept at the death of his friend Lazarus.
Lord, in your mercy:
℟. **Hear our prayer.**

For all of us assembled here to worship in faith, that we may be gathered together again in God's kingdom.
Lord, in your mercy:
℟. **Hear our prayer.**

B

*The priest begins:*

My dear friends, let us join with one another in praying to God, not only for our departed brother/sister, but also for the Church, for peace in the world, and for ourselves.

*A deacon or reader then continues:*

That the bishops and priests of the Church, and all who preach the Gospel, may be given the strength to express in action the word they proclaim.
We pray to the Lord:
℞. **Lord, hear our prayer.**

That those in public office may promote justice and peace.
We pray to the Lord:
℞. **Lord, hear our prayer.**

That those who bear the cross of pain in mind or body may never feel forsaken by God.
We pray to the Lord:
℞. **Lord, hear our prayer.**

That God may deliver the soul of his servant N. from punishment and from the powers of darkness.
We pray to the Lord:
℞. **Lord, hear our prayer.**

That God in his mercy may blot out all his/her offences.
We pray to the Lord:
℞. **Lord, hear our prayer.**

That God may establish him/her in light and peace.
We pray to the Lord:
℞. **Lord, hear our prayer.**

That God may call him/her to happiness in the company of all the saints.
We pray to the Lord:
℞. **Lord, hear our prayer.**

That God may welcome into his glory those of our family and friends who have departed this life.
We pray to the Lord:
℞. **Lord, hear our prayer.**

That God may give a place in the kingdom of heaven to all the faithful departed.
We pray to the Lord:
℞. **Lord, hear our prayer.**

# The Final Commendation

*The Commendation comes near the end of the funeral, after communion if Mass has been celebrated. It is the moment when the relatives, friends and the whole Church say farewell to the one who has died and commend him or her to the mercy and love of God.*

*The priest or minister goes to a place near the coffin and invites those present to pray (see this page). This is followed by a short silence, and the **Song of Farewell** (p.76). Holy water may be sprinkled on the coffin and incense burnt. Finally there is the **Prayer of Commendation** (p.77). If the committal is to take place somewhere else, there is a procession out of church during which there may be singing (p.79).*

## Invitation to the Prayers of Commendation

A    Before we go our separate ways, let us take leave of our brother/sister. May our farewell express our affection for him/her; may it ease our sadness and strengthen our hope. One day we shall joyfully greet him/her again when the love of Christ, which conquers all things, destroys even death itself.

B    Trusting in God, we have prayed together for N. and now we come to the last farewell. There is sadness in parting, but we take comfort in the hope that one day we shall see N. again and enjoy his/her friendship. Although this congregation will disperse in sorrow, the mercy of God will gather us together again in the joy of his kingdom. Therefore let us console one another in the faith of Jesus Christ.

C    Our brother/sister N. has fallen asleep in Christ. Confident in our hope of eternal life, let us commend him/her to the loving mercy of our Father and let our prayers go with him/her. He/she was adopted as God's son/daughter in baptism and was nourished at the table of the Lord; may he/she now inherit the promise of eternal life and take his/her place at the table of God's children in heaven.

Let us pray also on our own behalf, that we who now mourn and are saddened may one day go forth with our brother/sister to meet the Lord of life when he appears in glory.

D    *This prayer is for use at a burial, not at a cremation.*

With faith in Jesus Christ, we must reverently bury the body of our brother/sister.

Let us pray with confidence to God, in whose sight all creation lives, that he will raise up in holiness and power the mortal body of our brother/sister and command his/her soul to be numbered among the blessed.

May God grant him/her a merciful judgment, deliverance from death, and pardon of sin. May Christ the Good Shepherd carry him/her home to be at peace with the Father. May he/she rejoice for ever in the presence of the eternal King and in the company of all the saints.

E      *This prayer is for use at a burial, not at a cremation.*

Because God has chosen to call our brother/sister N. from this life to himself, we commit his/her body to the earth, for we are dust and unto dust we shall return.

But the Lord Jesus Christ will change our mortal bodies to be like his in glory, for he is risen, the first-born from the dead.

So let us commend our brother/sister to the Lord, that the Lord may embrace him/her in peace and raise up his/her body on the last day.

# For children

A      **A baptized child**

God in his wisdom knows the span of our days; he has chosen to call to himself this child, whom he adopted as his own in baptism. The body of N. will one day rise again to a new and radiant life that will never end.

Our firm belief is that N., because he/she was baptized, has already entered this new life; our firm hope is that we shall do the same. Let us ask God to comfort his/her family and friends and to increase our desire for the joys of heaven.

B      **A baptized child**

With faith in Jesus Christ, we bid farewell to N. Let us pray with confidence to God, in whose sight all creation lives, that he will raise up in holiness and power the mortal body of this [little] child, for God has chosen to number him/her among the blessed.

C      **A child who died before baptism**

Let us commend this child/baby to the Lord's merciful keeping; and let us pray with all our hearts for N. and N. Even as they grieve at the loss of their [little] child, they entrust him/her to the loving embrace of God.

# Songs of Farewell

*This song allows those present to commend their loved one to God. There are other Songs of Farewell besides those given here (see page 22); the priest or organist should be able to give some suggestions.*

A      I know that my Redeemer lives,
And on that final day of days,
His voice shall bid me rise again:
Unending joy, unceasing praise!

This hope I cherish in my heart:
To stand on earth, my flesh restored,
And, not a stranger but a friend,
Behold my Saviour and my Lord.

B     Saints of God, come to his/her aid!
Hasten to meet him/her, angels of the Lord!
> **Receive his/her soul and present him/her
> to God the Most High.**

May Christ, who called you, take you to himself;
may angels lead you to the bosom of Abraham.
> **Receive his/her soul and present him/her
> to God the Most High.**

Eternal rest grant unto him/her, O Lord,
and let perpetual light shine upon him/her.
> **Receive his/her soul and present him/her
> to God the Most High.**

# Prayers of commendation

*This is the final prayer of the service in church, in which the priest or minister, in the
name of the community, commends the dead person to the love of God.*

A   Into your hands, Father of mercies,
we commend our brother/sister N.
in the sure and certain hope
that, together with all who have died in Christ,
he/she will rise with him on the last day.

[We give you thanks for the blessings
which you bestowed upon N. in this life:
they are signs to us of your goodness
and of our fellowship with the saints in
    Christ.]
Merciful Lord, turn toward us and listen
    to our prayers:
open the gates of paradise to your servant
and help us who remain
to comfort one another with assurances
    of faith,
until we all meet in Christ
and are with you and with our brother/
    sister for ever.

We ask this through Christ our Lord.
**Amen.**

B   To you, O Lord, we commend the soul
    of N., your servant;
in the sight of this world he/she is now dead;
In your sight may he/she live for ever.
Forgive whatever sins he/she committed
    through human weakness
and in your goodness grant him/her ever-
    lasting peace.

We ask this through Christ our Lord.
**Amen.**

# Prayer of Commendation for Children

A    **A baptized child**

You are the author and sustainer of our
    lives, O God.
You are our final home.
We commend to you N., our child/baby.

In baptism he/she began his/her journey
    toward you.
Take him/her now to yourself
and give him/her the life
promised to those born again of water
    and the Spirit.

Turn also to us who have suffered this loss
Strengthen the bonds of this family and
    our community.
Confirm us in faith, in hope, and in love,
so that we may bear your peace to one
    another
and one day stand together with all the saints
who praise you for your saving help.

We ask this in the name of your Son,
whom you raised from among the dead,
Jesus Christ, our Lord.
**Amen.**

B    **A baptized child**

Lord Jesus,
 like a shepherd who gathers the lambs
to protect them from all harm,
you led N. to the waters of baptism
and shielded him/her in innocence.

Now carry this little one
on the path to your kingdom of light
where he/she will find happiness
and every tear will be wiped away.

To you be glory, now and for ever.
**Amen.**

C    **A baptized child**

Into your gentle keeping, O Lord,
we commend this child [N.].
Though our hearts are troubled,
we hope in your loving kindness.

By the sign of the cross
he/she was claimed for Christ,
and in the waters of baptism
he/she died with Christ to live in him
    for ever.

May the angels, our guardians,
lead N. now to paradise
where your saints will welcome him/her
and every tear will be wiped away.
There we shall join in songs of praise for
    ever.

We ask this through Christ our Lord.
**Amen.**

D    **A child who died before baptism**

You are the author and sustainer of our
    lives, O God,
you are our final home.
We commend to you N., our child/baby.

Trusting in your mercy
and in your all-embracing love,
we pray that you give him/her happiness
    for ever.

Turn also to us who have suffered this loss.
Strengthen the bonds of this family and
    our community.
Confirm us in faith, in hope, and in love,
so that we may bear your peace to one
    another
and one day stand together with all the saints
who praise you for your saving help.

We ask this in the name of your Son,
    Jesus Christ, our Lord.
**Amen.**

# Procession to the place of committal

*At the end of the church service the priest or minister says:*

In peace let us carry N. to his/her place of rest.

*There follows a procession out of church, which may continue all the way to the place of committal if that is near. During this procession one of the following may be sung (see also page 22).*

A        **Psalm 24 (p.34) with the refrain**

May the angels lead you into paradise;
may the martyrs come to welcome you
and take you to the holy city,
the new and eternal Jerusalem.

B        **Psalm 114 (p.36) with the refrain**

May choirs of angels welcome you
and lead you to the bosom of Abraham;
and where Lazarus is poor no longer
may you find eternal rest.

C

May saints and angels lead you on,
escorting you where Christ has gone.
Now he has called you, come to him
who sits above the seraphim.

Come to the peace of Abraham
and to the supper of the Lamb:
come to the glory of the blessed,
and to perpetual light and rest.

# The Rite of Committal

*The prayers and texts for this rite will be found on the following pages:*

## Prayers over the place of committal: for a burial

*Prayers for a cremation, see p.82*

A   All praise to you, Lord of all creation.
Praise to you, holy and living God.
We praise and bless you for your mercy,
we praise and bless you for your kindness.
Blessed is the Lord, our God.
**Blessed is the Lord, our God.**

You sanctify the homes of the living
and make holy the places of the dead.
You alone open the gates of righteousness
and lead us to the dwellings of the saints.
Blessed is the Lord, our God.
**Blessed is the Lord, our God.**

We praise you, our refuge and strength.
We bless you, our God and Redeemer.
Your praise is always in our hearts and
    on our lips.
We remember the mighty deeds of the
    covenant.
Blessed is the Lord, our God.
**Blessed is the Lord, our God.**

Almighty and ever-living God,
remember the mercy with which you
    graced your servant N. in life.
Receive him/her, we pray, into the
    mansions of the saints.
As we make ready our brother's/sister's
    resting place,
look also with favour on those who mourn
    and comfort them in their loss.
Grant this through Christ our Lord.
**Amen.**

B   **If the place of committal is to be blessed**

Lord Jesus Christ,
by your own three days in the tornb,
you hallowed the graves of all who believe in
    you
and so made the grave a sign of hope
that promises resurrection
even as it claims our mortal bodies.

Grant that our brother/sister may sleep here
    in peace
until you awaken him/her to glory,
for you are the resurrection and the life.
Then he/she will see you face to face
and in your light will see light
and know the splendour of God,
for you live and reign for ever and ever.
**Amen.**

C   **If the place of committal is to be blessed**

O God,
by whose mercy the faithful departed find
    rest,
bless this grave,
and send your holy angel to watch over it.
As we bury here the body of our
    brother/sister,
deliver his/her soul from every bond of sin,
that he/she may rejoice in you with your
    saints for ever.
We ask this through Christ our Lord.
**Amen.**

D **If the place of committal is to be blessed**

Almighty God,
you created the earth and shaped the vault
   of heaven;
you fixed the stars in their places.
When we were caught in the snares of death
you set us free through baptism;
in obedience to your will
our Lord Jesus Christ
broke the fetters of hell and rose to life,
bringing deliverance and resurrection
to those who are his by faith.
In your mercy look upon this grave,
so that your servant may sleep here in peace;
and on the day of judgment raise him/her up
to dwell with your saints in paradise.

We ask this through Christ our Lord.
**Amen.**

E **If the place of committal is to be blessed**

God of endless ages,
through disobedience to your law
we fell from grace
and death entered the world;
but through the obedience and resurrection
   of your Son
you revealed to us a new life.
You granted Abraham, our father in faith,
a burial place in the promised land;
you prompted Joseph of Arimathea
to offer his own tomb for the burial of the
   Lord.
In a spirit of repentance
we earnestly ask you to look upon this grave
   and bless it,
so that, while we commit to the earth/its
   resting place
the body of your servant N.
his/her soul may be taken into paradise.

We ask this through Christ our Lord.
**Amen.**

# Prayers over the place of committal: for children

A  All praise to you, Lord of all creation.
   Praise to you, holy and living God.
   We praise and bless you for your mercy,
   we praise and bless you for your kindness.
   Blessed is the Lord, our God.
   **Blessed is the Lord, our God.**

You sanctify the homes of the living
and make holy the places of the dead.
You alone open the gates of righteousness
and lead us to the dwellings of the saints.
Blessed is the Lord, our God.
**Blessed is the Lord, our God.**

We praise you, our refuge and strength.
We bless you, our God and Redeemer.
Your praise is always in our hearts
   and on our lips.

We remember the mighty deeds of the
   covenant.
Blessed is the Lord, our God.
**Blessed is the Lord, our God.**

Almighty and ever-living God,
remember the mercy with which you graced
   your child N. in  [his/her short]life.
Receive him/her, we pray, into the
   mansions of the saints.
As we make ready this resting place,
look also with favour on those who mourn
and comfort them in their loss.
Grant this through Christ our Lord.
**Amen.**

81

B  Almighty and ever-living God,
   in you we place our trust and hope,
   in you the dead, whose bodies were
        temples of the Spirit,
   find everlasting peace.

   As we take leave of N.,
   give our hearts peace in the firm hope
   that one day he/she will live
   in the mansion you have prepared for
        him/her in heaven.

   We ask this through Christ our Lord.
   **Amen.**

C  **If the place of committal is to be blessed**

   O God,
   by whose mercy the faithful departed
        find rest,
   bless this grave,
   and send your holy angel to watch over it.

   As we bury here the body of N.,
   welcome him/her into your presence,
   that he/she may rejoice in you with your
        saints for ever.

   We ask this through Christ our Lord.

   **Amen.**

## Prayers over the place of committal: for a cremation

A  Almighty and ever-living God,
   remember the love with which you
        graced your servant N. in life.
   Receive him/her, we pray, into the
        mansions of the saints.
   Look with favour on those who mourn
   and comfort them in their loss.

   Grant this through Christ our Lord.
   **Amen.**

B  Almighty and ever-living God,in you we
        place our trust and hope,
   in you the dead whose bodies were
        temples of the Spirit
   find everlasting peace.

   As we take leave of N.,
   give our hearts peace in the firm hope
   that one day he/she will live
   in the mansion you have prepared for
        him/her in heaven.

   We ask this through Christ our Lord.
   **Amen.**

### For children

A  Almighty and ever-living God,
   remember the love with which you
        graced your child N. in [his/her short] life.
   Receive him/her, we pray, into the
        mansions of the saints.
   Look with favour on those who mourn
   and comfort them in their loss.

   Grant this through Christ our Lord.
   **Amen.**

B  Almighty and ever-living God,
   in you we place our trust and hope,
   in you the dead, whose bodies were
        temples of the Spirit,
   find everlasting peace.

   As we take leave of N.,
   give our hearts peace in the firm hope
   that one day he/she will live
   in the mansion you have prepared for
        him/her in heaven.

   We ask this through Christ our Lord.
   **Amen.**

# Texts for committal: for a burial

*This is the prayer said just before or at the moment of burial.*

A    Because God has chosen to call our brother/sister N. from this life to himself,
we commit his/her body to [the earth/its resting place],
for we are dust and unto dust we shall return.

But the Lord Jesus Christ will change our mortal bodies to be like his in glory,
for he is risen, the firstborn from the dead.

So let us commend our brother/sister to the Lord,
that the Lord may embrace him/her in peace
and raise up his/her body on the last day.

B    In sure and certain hope of the resurrection to eternal life through our Lord Jesus Christ,
we commend to Almighty God our brother/sister N.,
and we commit his/her body to [the ground/its resting place]:
earth to earth, ashes to ashes, dust to dust.

The Lord bless him/her and keep him/her,
the Lord make his face to shine upon him/her and be gracious to him/her,
the Lord lift up his countenance upon him/her and give him/her peace.

# Texts for committal: for cremation

*This is the prayer said just before or just as the coffin is withdrawn from view.*

A    Because God has chosen to call our brother/sister N. from this life to himself,
we commit his/her body to be cremated
for we are dust and unto dust we shall return.

But the Lord Jesus Christ will change our mortal bodies to be like his in glory
for he is risen, the firstborn from the dead.

So let us commend our brother/sister to the Lord,
that the Lord may embrace him/her in peace
and raise up his/her body on the last day.

B    In sure and certain hope of the resurrection to eternal life through our Lord Jesus Christ,
we commend to Almighty God our brother/sister N.,
and we commit his/her body to be cremated:
earth to earth, ashes to ashes, dust to dust.

The Lord bless him/her and keep him/her,
the Lord make his face to shine upon him/her and be gracious to him/her,
the Lord lift up his countenance upon him/her and give him/her peace.

# Prayers for the committal of children

**A**      A baptized child

Into your hands, O merciful Saviour, we commend N.
Acknowledge, we humbly beseech you,
a sheep of your own fold, a lamb of your own flock.
Receive him/her into the arms of your mercy,
into the blessed rest of everlasting peace,
and into the glorious company of the saints in light.


**B**      A child who died before baptism

Lord God, ever-caring and gentle,
we commit to your love this little one [N.],
who brought joy to our lives for so short a time.
Enfold him/her in eternal life.

We pray for his/her parents
who are saddened by the loss of their child/baby.
Give them courage
and help them in their pain and grief.
May they all meet one day
in the joy and peace of your kingdom.

We ask this through Christ our Lord.
**Amen.**


# Prayer for the Burial of Ashes

Faithful God,
Lord of all creation,
you desire that nothing redeemed by your Son will ever be lost,
and that the just will be raised up on the last day.

Comfort us today with the word of your promise
as we return the ashes of our brother/sister to the earth.
Grant N. a place of rest and peace
where the world of dust and ashes has no dominion.
Confirm us in our hope that he/she will be created anew
on the day when you will raise him/her up in glory
to live with you and all the saints for ever and ever.
**Amen.**